BIAS-CUT DRESSMAKING

B.T. BATSFORD • LONDON

A catalogue record for this book is available from the British
Library.

ISBN 0 7134 8624 4

Printed and bound in Spain by Bookprint, S.L.,Barcelona

Volume © B T Batsford 2001

First published in 2001 by
B T Batsford
9 Blenheim Court
Brewery Road
London N7 9NY

A member of the Chrysalis Group plc

Front cover image: 1930s black crepe gown from the Irene Barnes collection at
Manor House Museum, Bury St Edmunds, Suffolk.

BIAS-CUT DRESSMAKING

Gillian Holman

Contents

Introduction

Bias-cut garments are surprisingly easy to cut and make, provided certain basic rules are followed in both the cut and construction.

The true bias is always 45 degrees from the straight grain of the fabric. One often sees a garment described as bias cut; strictly speaking this simply means that it is off grain. To hang properly it is essential that the true bias runs through the centre of the panel or in the case of some of the French knickers shown in the following pages, through the centre front and back of the garments.

In the instructions for some of the garments in this book, I have used the term true bias, and in other cases I have referred to the true bias as 45 degrees. This is done deliberately, in order to emphasize that the terms are interchangeable.

Sometimes one sees a bias-cut garment that does not hang properly. This indicates either that it has not been cut with the true bias through the centre of the panels or that it has been stitched incorrectly. The most obvious examples of the latter are found in men's neckties: if one holds a tie up by one end it should hang straight; if the tie spirals then it has either been stretched when stitched or cut incorrectly. It is essential to experiment with stitching before putting a garment together. Many fabrics will accept the use of an overlocking stitch to make the seams, and this generally works well with bias garments, as overlocking allows the stitch to stretch with the fabric. If an overlocker is not available, or if the fabric frays too much, use a very slight zigzag, which will also give with the fabric.

Most stretch stitches on domestic machines are too extreme for this type of work.

It is wise to stitch a zip into a bias-cut garment by hand, as the seamstress is less likely to stretch the fabric on to the zipper tape this way.

If a bias-cut garment includes sleeves, it is usual to cut these on the straight. A bias-cut sleeve in a dress that is entirely cut on the bias makes the stitching extremely difficult to control. Any sleeve that fits the original block should work in a bias-cut dress. When inserting a sleeve into this type of garment, it is wise to tape the shoulder and armhole seams to prevent stretch.

Metric and imperial measurements have been given with all instructions. It is easier to be more precise when working in millimetres and centimetres than in inches, and to avoid problems imperial measurements have been taken to the nearest ⅛ in.

Most of the designs for dresses and slips in the book are interchangeable and could serve either purpose. Where it is necessary to use neck and armhole facings, these should be traced off the final pattern and, apart from the cowl necks, cut on the straight grain, as this gives control to the garment

I have taught City and Guilds fashion students for many years and have often found that experienced dressmakers are frightened of cutting on the bias. As long as the rules are followed, the results are frequently stunning, and for lingerie and evening wear nothing is more effective or more comfortable than the combination of elegant drape and easy fit achieved by this method.

Basic Blocks for Pattern Cutting

Fitted Bodice Block

Personal measurements should be used for a bodice block. Those shown here are for a standard size 12. Add ease to all horizontal measurements before drawing out the pattern.

1. Bust	88 cm + 5 cm ease = 93 cm (34⅝ in + 2 in = 36⅝ in)
2. Waist	68 cm + 2.5 cm ease (26¾ in + 1 in)
3. Hip	93 cm + 5 cm ease (36⅝ in + 2 in)
4. Cross back	34.4 cm + 2 cm ease (13½ in + ¾ in)
5. Cross chest	32.4 cm + 2 cm ease (12¾ in + ¾ in)
6. Neck	38 cm + 2 cm ease (15 in + ¾ in)
7. Total front dart	7 cm (2¾in)
8. CF neck to waist	35 cm + 1 cm ease (13¾ in + ⅜ in)
9. Front shoulder to waist	45 cm + 1 cm ease (17¾ in + ⅜ in)
10. Back shoulder to waist	45 cm + 2 cm ease(17¾ in + ¾ in)
11. CB neck to waist	40 cm + 2 cm ease (15¾ in + ¾ in)
12. Shoulder length	12.25 cm + 1 cm ease (4⅞+ ⅜ in)
13. Top arm to elbow	30 cm + 2 cm ease (12 in + ¾ in)
14. Armhole depth	21 cm + 2 cm ease (8¼ in + ¾ in)
15. Hip depth	20 cm + 1 cm ease (8 in + ⅜ in)

Bodice Draft

Back Bodice and Neck

0-1   Back shoulder to waist
0-2   Half bust including ease: for example, 88 cm +
         5 cm ease = 93 cm (34⅝ in + 2 in = 36⅝ in);
         divide by 2 = 46.5 cm (18⅜ in)
2-3   Equals 0-1 (Square down to 3 and across to 1)
0-4   2 cm (¾ in)
0-5   One fifth of neck measurement
4-5   Neck curve
4-6   2.5 cm (1 in) down, then rule at right angle
         across for 25 cm (9⅞ in)
5-7   Shoulder length, measured from 5 to line from
         6
7-8   Armhole depth; square across both ways to 9
         and 10
9-10 Underarm line; square out both ways from 8
11   Half depth 7-8; square out to centre back line
12   Half cross-back measurement on line from 11
2-13 One-fifth of neck measurement less 1 cm
         (⅜ in)
2-14 Equals 2-13 + 1.5 cm (⅝ in)
2-15 Equals 2-13 + 5 mm (¼ in), taking
         measurement diagonally from 2. Join 13-14-15
         for neck curve.
16   Half of 1-3
17   Square up from 16 to line 9-10
18-19 Half of line 8-9 squared down to line 1-3.
For a semi-fitted back dart, mark a dart 1.5 cm (⅝ in)
         on each side of 19 and take off to nothing at
         18.
Draw in the armhole from 7 to 12 to 17.

Front Bodice Shaping

Square across the block for 20 cm (7⅞ in) from 15.
13-20 Shoulder length + 4 cm (1⅝ in) dart
21   Half shoulder line 13-20
22   4 cm (1⅝ in) towards neckline from 21
14-23 Bust point level, measure down from centre
         front neck, which is usually approximately 3cm
         (1⅛ in) below armhole. Square out across
         bodice.
24   Half measurement 10-14
25   Square across from 24 to half cross-chest
         measurement including ease plus whatever the
         dart measures on this line.
26   Square down from 25 to line 9-10.
27   Half measurement of line 10-26 on line from
         23. For the dart, rule back to 21 and 22 on the
         shoulder. Fold out the dart and correct
         shoulder line to incorporate the top of the
         dart.
28   Square down from 27 and mark out 1.5 cm
         (⅝ in) on each side for the dart. Mark in
         armhole from 20 to 25 to 17.

Side Shaping

For side shaping, mark up 1.5 cm (⅝ in) from 16 and
         curve back to front and back darts. Mark out
         1.5 cm (⅝ in) on each side of 16 and rule back to
         nothing at 17 for a semi-fitted side seam.

For sleeveless styles, raise the underarm curve by
         approximately 1.5 cm (⅝ in) to prevent gape
         showing the edge of the bra.

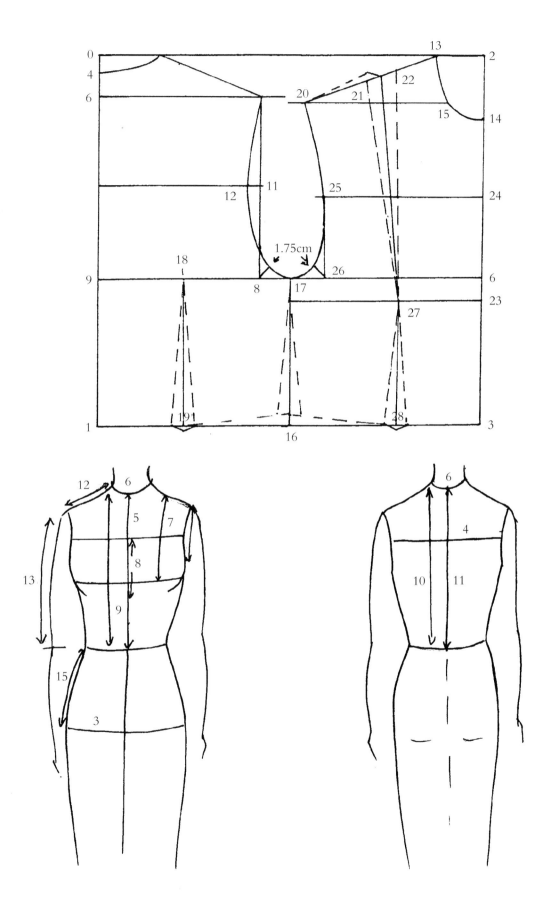

Hip Length Block

1   Outline the front and back bodice blocks and extend at centre front and centre back lines by the hip depth.
2   From centre front and centre back lines, square across by a quarter of the hip measurement including ease.
3   Join waist to hip at the side seam (see dotted line). Soften the waist shaping from point A through the waist, and curve gently over the hip.
4   Extend the under-bust dart to approximately 3 cm (1⅛ in) above the hip level, and reduce the dart width by half. This prevents unsightly creasing caused by the garment being too tightly fitted through the waist.

Lingerie Block

1   Outline a *fitted* front and back bodice block and extend this to a hip block.
2   Extend back and front blocks to knee length.

Front

3   Mark cross-chest line on front block, **fig 1**. Mark parallel line 10 cm (4 in) down for top of block.
4   Draw in bust line through bust point.
5   Raise waist line at centre front block by 15 mm (⅝ in) and curve down to natural centre back point (dotted line, **fig 1**).
6   Adjust widest area of dart to new waistline.
7   Mark in top hip line, across hip bones – approximately 10 cm (4 in) below waist.
8   Lower armhole by 1.5 cm (⅝ in) on back and front blocks.
9   Reduce front and back blocks as follows (see dotted line):
at side seam underarm take off 6 mm (¼ in),
at bust line take off 5 mm (¼ in),
at waistline take off 6 mm (¼ in),
at hipline take off 3 mm (⅛ in).
10   Join new side seams without sharp angles and drop straight down from hip to hem.
11   Increase bust dart at shoulder by a third on each side and draw back to bust point (see dotted lines). If stitched down this will give closer fit across top of bust.

12   From centre front square out to dart line 1.5cm (⅝ in) below cross-chest line.
13   Measure the length of the dart stitching line from A to B.
14   Mark the other dart stitching line the same length from bust point (C), and angle down from A to C.
15   Gently curve from dart to underarm. Square off at top of dart and cut away along line.

Back

16   Lower the armhole to match front block at the side seam, **fig 2.** Curve down approximately 3 cm (⅛ in) from underarm line and then straight across to centre back. This usually cuts across the top point of the back dart. Cut away on this line.
17   If the back dart is longer and cutting away on this line removes the dart point, ignore the shaping and take off any excess width at the side seam.
18   For an A-line garment approximately 2.5 cm (1 in) at back and front should be added to side seams at hem and ruled back to nothing at hip.
19   If creating a princess line, use dart line and shaping for princess seaming (see Classic princess-line petticoat).
20   Cut away only half of waist dart shaping to give comfortable but elegant fit. For extra ease at hem, add fullness at hem on all panels and rule back to nothing at hip.
21   For final pattern, place CF line on fold of paper and cut, open out to whole front and whole back, **fig 4.** True bias to CF and CB.
22   If a dartless front is wanted, ignore darts and curve in side seam as follows: on front take off 1 cm (scant ½ in) at underarm and curve back to bust line.
23   On back, take off 5 mm (¼ in) at underarm and curve back to bust level.
24   Any additional fullness may be disposed of by applying binding or lace trim and easing garment top on to this.
25   Across the top hip line, approximately 10 cm (4 in) below the waist and across the hip bones, draw the *camisole line.*

Fitted Evening Wear

The Lingerie block is suitable for close-fitting
   evening wear, but the following adjustments
   must be made: bring waistline back to normal
   level and then at centre back lower the waist by
   1.5 cm (⅝ in) and curve back to side seam.

HIP BLOCK

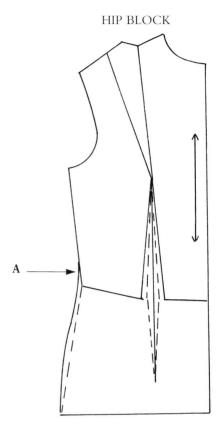

A →

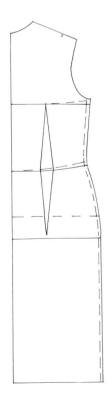

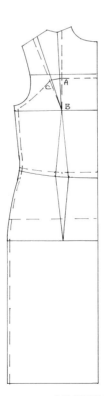

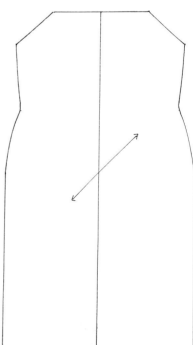

LINGERIE BLOCKS

Basic Briefs Block

For all briefs and knickers, complete the pattern as instructed, adding extra depth for elastic casing only when everything else is done.

1 Measure crotch depth: sit in a hard upright chair and measure from the seat of the chair to your waist level. This is the crotch depth or body rise.

2 Draw a vertical line the depth of the crotch and mark A at the top and B at the bottom. Square out each side of A for one quarter of waist measurement plus 7 mm (⅝ in). For example, if waist is 68 cm (26½ in) a quarter of this equals 17 cm (6⅝ in). The line each side of A must measure 17.7 cm (7¼ in). Mark this line CD, **fig 1.**

3 Measure down to hip line (the widest point around the seat, not the hip bone) and square out each side of line AB at this point by a quarter of the hip plus 7.5 mm (⅝ in). Mark this line EF, **fig 1.**

4 At crotch level, square out 5 cm (2 in) on one side of line AB for the back, and 4 cm (1½ in) on the other side of line AB for the front. Mark this line G for the back and H for the front, **fig 1.**

5 Join waist to hip to crotch: C to E to G and D to F to H.

6 On line from hip to crotch, curve front leg up by 2 cm (¾ in) and on back hip to crotch line curve down by 1.5 cm (⅝ in), **fig 1.**

7 Cut apart down line AB; this gives separate front and back patterns. Label cut lines CF (centre front) and CB (centre back) respectively.

8 Trace off front pattern with CF line to fold of paper, and open out to full pattern, **fig 2.** When cutting the garment, cut one front with the grain line at 45 degrees from the CF.

9 For back pattern slash and spread on hip line from CB to side seam and swing down lower section by approximately 2 cm (⅞ in). Curve out on CB line by 2 cm (⅞ in), see dashed line, **fig 3.** Redraw with true bias at 45 degrees from original CB line. When cutting garment, cut two, **fig 4.** This method gives room for the curve of the seat.

10 For stretch fabrics, CB and CF lines may be used as straight grain and cut on fold of fabric.

11 For the gusset, draw vertical line 10 cm (4 in) for smaller sizes, 13 cm (5⅛ in) for larger sizes; mark this JK. At J, square out at both sides the width of the crotch – 4 cm (1½ in) – on the front pattern, and at K for the width of the back pattern – 5 cm (2 in). Join the top to the bottom horizontals with a straight line and curve in, say 1 cm (scant ½ in) about halfway along for a comfortable gusset, **fig 5.** When making up, line this section with stretch cotton.

12 Put in balance marks (notches) on side seams and gusset seams.

Sample Measurements

For a standard size 12: a quarter of waist measuring 68 cm (26¾ in) equals 17 cm (6⅝ in). Add 7 mm (⅝ in) to make total length of line CD 35.4 cm (13¼ in)
A quarter of hip measuring 93 cm (36⅝ in) equals 23.25 cm (9⅛ in). Add 7 mm (⅝ in) to make total length of line EF 48 cm (18⅞ in).

These instructions are for a standard waist high brief which give a smooth line under a fitted skirt or trousers. Many people, however, prefer either a brief cut high over the leg or cut lower over the hip. The following basic instructions should be used for either adaptation before cutting the pattern for the garment. It is useful to keep a block pattern of both basic shapes.

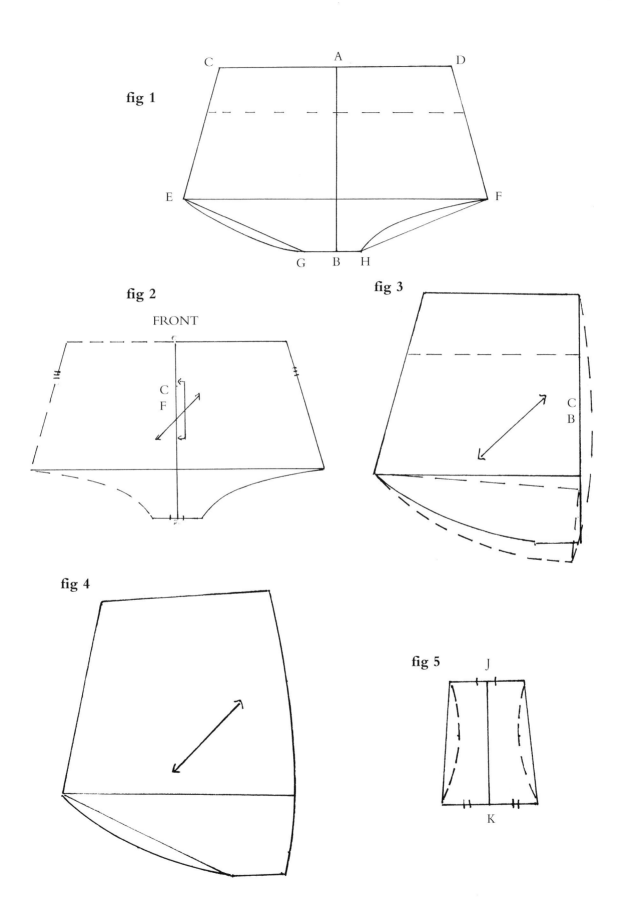

fig 1

fig 2

FRONT

fig 3

fig 4

fig 5

Camiknickers, Basic Block

This is a case of marrying two patterns, a camisole block cropped to the waist is joined to French knickers.

Front

1 Outline the lingerie blocks to the waist, **fig 1.**
2 Extend the CF and CB lines.
3 Place the CF of the French knicker pattern against the line, meeting but not overlapping the bodice block, **fig 1.**
4 Remember that the knicker patterns were straightened at the hip to allow for elastic, if this means that the pattern extends beyond the bodice at the side seam, adjust slightly as needed, see broken line, **fig 1.**
5 Redraw the pattern and shape off slightly at the side seam to allow for removal of dart shaping if a closer fit is wanted, **fig 2.**

Back

6 Outline lingerie back to waist as instructed for the front, **fig 3.**
7 Extend the CB line and place the CB French knicker pattern against this, meeting but not overlapping the bodice at the waist, **fig 3.**
8 Adjust on the side seam as needed for the style required, see broken lines, **fig 3.**

Gusset

9 The gusset should be cut as instructed for French knickers, **fig 4a.**
10 Sometimes the 1930s camiknickers were joined to the gusset at back and front, **fig 4b.** However if an opening is preferred join the gusset to the garment at the back crotch, and add a button wrap to the unattached edge to fasten to the front, **fig 4a**.

fig 1

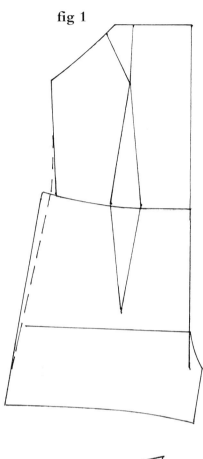

fig 2

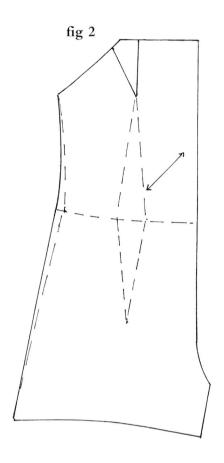

fig 3

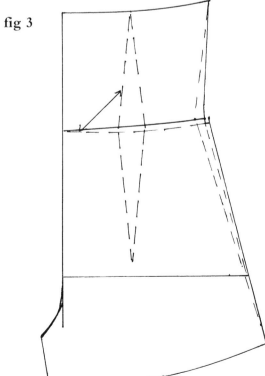

fig 4a

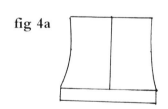

fig 4b

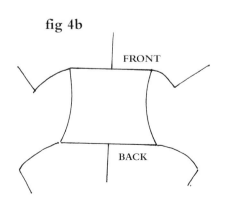

FRONT

BACK

Basic Block for a 'Body' or Teddy

For this popular and useful garment it is necessary to marry the camisole block to the briefs block at the top hip or camisole line.

Front and Back

1 Outline the lingerie front and back blocks down to the camisole line, **figs 1 and 2**.

2 Take the basic briefs block and with the CF line continuing from the CF of the camisole pattern, place the two pattern pieces together on the top hip line, draw the briefs on as shown in the solid lines, **figs 1 and 2**.

3 Extend at the crotch by 5 cm (2 in), and mark broken line back to side seam/leg, **figs 1 and 2**.

4 If a high leg is wanted, curve back to the required level, **figs 1 and 2**.

5 Check that patterns match at the side seam.

6 Draw in the bust dart on the front pattern and dot in the waist darts on front and back, **figs 1 and 2**.

7 For the gusset pattern, follow instructions for the basic brief gusset, adding a button wrap. This should be attached to the garment back at the crotch and fastens to the front with small plastic poppers. Add a small button stand to the front of the gusset. As with briefs, the gusset should be lined with stretch cotton.

This is the basic shape from which a fitted body is cut. The dart shaping can be utilized in style lines if needed. Generally the garment does not require a tight fit around the waist.

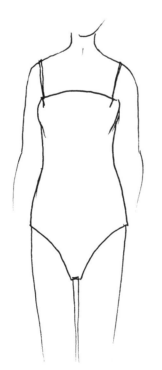
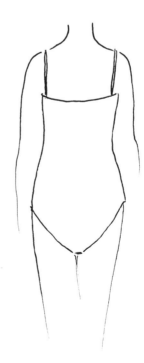

fig 1

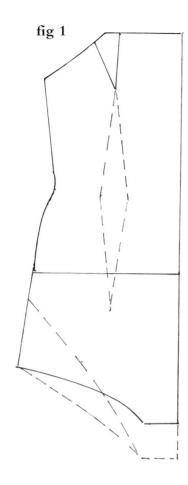

fig 2

Basic Skirt Block

Take accurate measurements for the waist (at the narrowest part of the body), hip (the widest part of the body, *not* the hip-bone level), hip depth (from waist to hip at the side seam), skirt length (waist to knee) and waist to floor.

Add the following to the body measurements for ease before dividing for a quarter pattern: 5-6 cm (2–2⅜ in) at hip, and 2.5 cm (1 in) at waist.

Skirt Back

A-B   Skirt length from waist to knee

A-C   Hip depth

C-D   Quarter of hip measurement including ease. For hip of 93 cm (36⅝ in), add 5 cm (2 in) ease. Quarter of 98 cm (38⅝ in) = 24.5 cm (9⅝ in).

B-E   Equals C-D

E-F   Equals A-B

A-G   Quarter of waist measurement including ease + 3 cm (1⅛ in) dart (4 cm [1⅝ in] for size 16 and above, or for a very small waist).

G-H   1.25 cm (½ in) up from line A-F

A-H   Waist line curve. Lower at C-B by 1 cm (⅜ in) and curve up at the side seam.

H-D   Draw a straight line from H to D. Mark out 1 cm (⅜ in) at centre and curve for hips.

For sizes 10/12/14, mark a dart 10/11/12 cm (4/4⅜ /4¾ in) along the waist from point A. For larger sizes, move the dart out towards the hip by 6mm (¼ in) per size. Draw a vertical line to the level of the hipbone, approximately 12-13 cm (4¾–5⅛ in), and mark 1.5 cm (⅝ in) on each side of this for a dart for smaller sizes. If the dart is too large to fit smoothly, divide to make two smaller darts. For larger sizes, draw a dart 2 cm (¾ in) on each side of this line. At point E, the side seam/hem, mark up 5 mm (¼ in) and curve the hem.

Skirt Front

Trace off the skirt back and shorten the darts from their point by approximately 2 cm (¾ in). Raise at the centre front by 5 mm (¼ in) and take off to nothing at the side seam (see broken line). Adjust to new waistline.

If the wearer has a large stomach, take 5 mm (¼ in) from the front side seam and extend back by 5 mm (¼ in). Reverse the procedure for a large bottom.

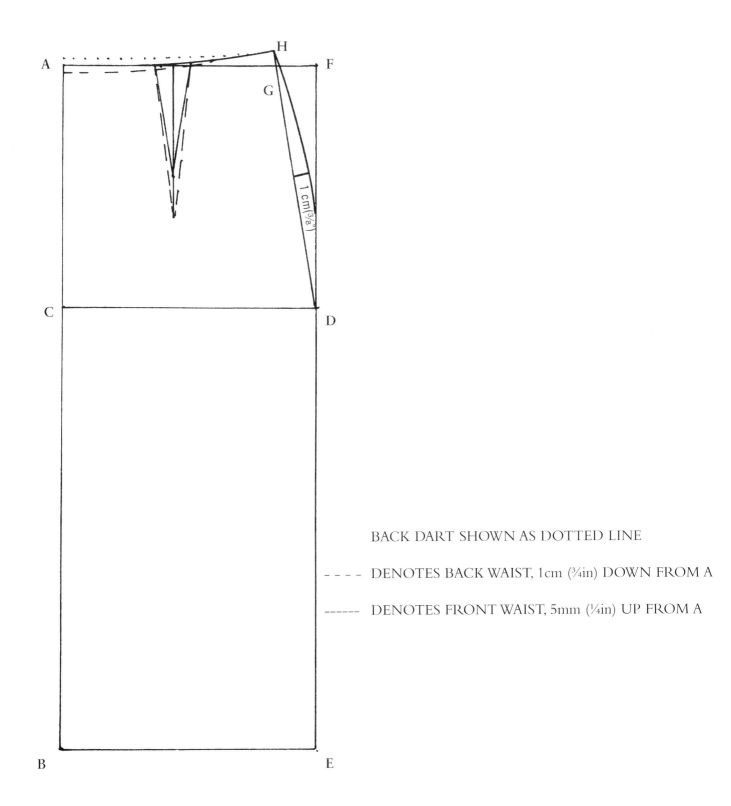

1 cm(⅜")

BACK DART SHOWN AS DOTTED LINE

- - - - DENOTES BACK WAIST, 1cm (⅜in) DOWN FROM A

------ DENOTES FRONT WAIST, 5mm (¼in) UP FROM A

Briefs and Knickers

High-leg Briefs

1   Trace off basic brief shape as above.
2   On side seam lines CE and DF, draw in the leg style line at height required and follow steps 5 and 6 as above, **figs 6 and 7.**

Hip Level Briefs

1   Take the crotch depth measurement as outlined in the basic brief block.
2   Take the measurement down from the waist to the top hip, across the hip bones and (usually) about 10 cm (4 in) below the waist.
3   Measure the top hip girth of the wearer and then follow the instructions for basic briefs from step 3 onwards, **figs 8 and 9.**

CLASSIC BRIEF FROM BASIC BLOCK

HIP-LEVEL BRIEF

HIGH LEG BRIEF

fig 6

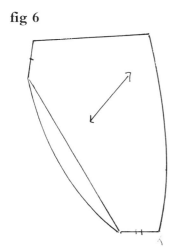

fig 7

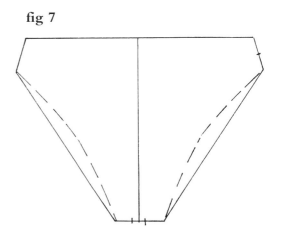

fig 9

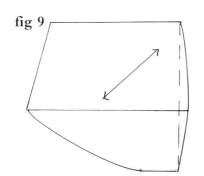

fig 8

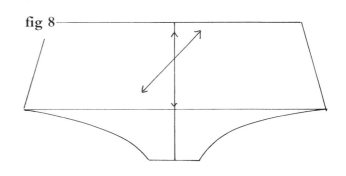

Cutaway Briefs

Cutaway briefs are made with a separate waistband, which should be of double-edged stretch lace trim. If stretch trim is not available, use double-edged lace trim and ease on to soft elastic. This is most easily achieved by measuring the elastic around the girth of the body, ensuring it is wide enough to slide on and off comfortably. This should then be stretched on to the underside of the lace trim.

Front

1   Outline high-leg brief block and then lower upper edge by approximately 8 to 10 cm (3½ to 4 in), see broken line, **fig 1.**
2   Cut away on broken line and draw grain at 45 degrees from CF line, **fig 2.**

Back

3   Outline high-leg brief back block and lower upper edge to match front pattern at side seam, **fig 3.**
4   Cut away on broken line and draw in grain at 45 degrees from the CB, **fig 4.** Cut two and join down CB.

Gusset

5   Cut as instructed for basic briefs and join to back and front sections. Join front and back of the garment to the gusset and trim before adding waist trim.

Waist

6   Mark the centre back and the centre front on the waist lace; match these to CB and CF on the front and back of the garment, and attach, stretching the elastic slightly over front and back for a flatter appearance over tummy and seat.

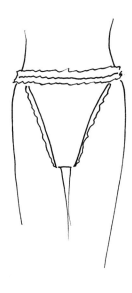

fig 1

fig 2

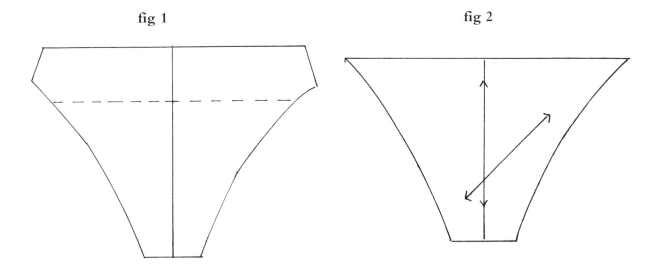

fig 3

fig 4

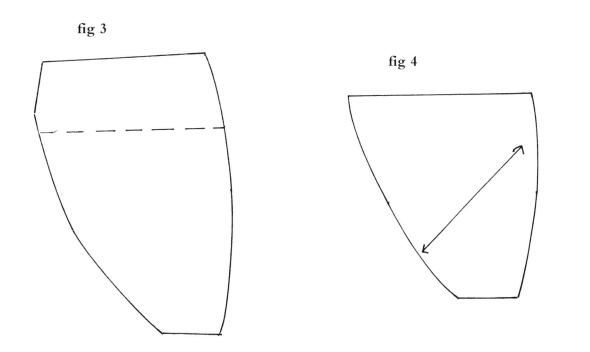

High-cut French Knickers

These simple French knickers are cut from a briefs block. Use either the high-cut leg block or the standard briefs.

Front

1 Outline block and extend at side seam as required for the design, draw back with slight curve to crotch line, see broken line, **fig 1.**
2 Divide into three at the waist and at the leg (do not include the crotch line in this), see broken lines, **fig 2.**
3 Slash and spread from leg to waist to give extra fullness to leg, **fig 2.**
4 Redraw the leg curve, see broken line, **fig 3.**
5 Trace off for final pattern, with CF to fold of pattern paper. Open out to full front and draw in grain line at 45 degrees from CF, **fig 4.**

Back

6 Outline back block and adjust at side seam to match front pattern, see broken line, **fig 5.**
7 Divide into three at waist and leg, as for front, see vertical broken lines, **fig 5.**
8 Slash and spread as for front, **fig 6.**
9 Trace off and put in grain line at 45 degrees from original CB, **fig 7.** Cut two.

Add casing for elastic to upper edges only when the pattern is complete, and cut the gusset as for basic briefs.

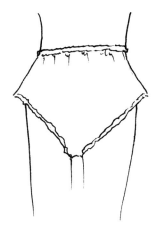
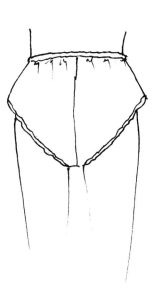

fig 1

fig 3

fig 2

fig 4

fig 5

fig 6

fig 7

French Knickers – Method One

1 Draw a vertical line the crotch depth plus 2 cm (¾ in). Mark this AB, **fig 1.**
2 Square out at waist, hip and crotch as for basic briefs block. Mark waist line CD, hip line EF and crotch line GH, **fig 1.**
3 At side seam on lines CE and DF, extend below hip by approximately 5 cm (2 in). Do not go below level of crotch. Draw straight line from side seams to crotch and curve front leg up by approximately 2 cm (⅞ in). Curve back leg down by the same amount, dashed lines **fig 1.**
4 From D to A, curve waist line down by approximately 1 cm (scant ½ in), see broken line, **fig 1.**
5 Cut away the front pattern from the back down line AB.

Front

6 Trace off front pattern and measure width across the panel at the waist and between the centre front and side seam. Mark a centre line, **fig 2.**
7 Mark grain at 45 degrees from this line. Put in balance marks, **fig 2.**

Back

8 Slash and spread across hip line from CB, swinging lower section down by 2 cm (¾ in). Curve out slightly on CB line – approximately 2 cm (¾ in), depending on size of the seat – see broken lines, **fig 3.**
9 Mark the centre line of the panel and put in grain line at 45 degrees as for front. Put in balance marks, **fig 4.**
10 Cut the gusset as for basic briefs and add casing for elastic at waist.

fig 1

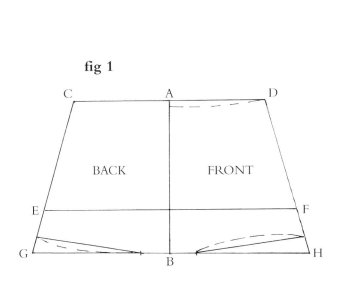

fig 2

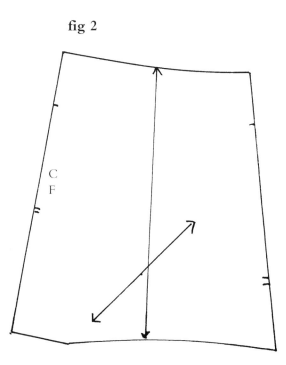

fig 3

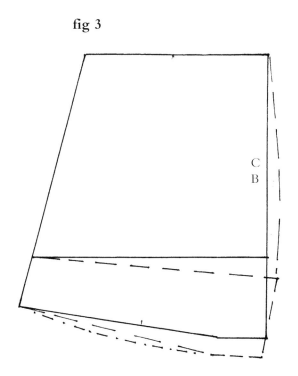

fig 4

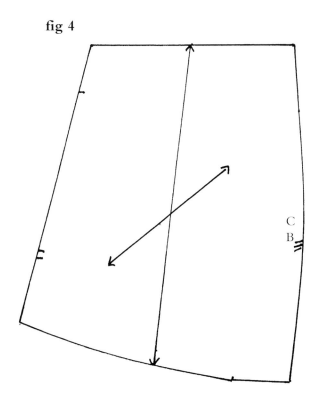

French Knickers – Method Two

Front

1 Trace off any well-cut trouser pattern.
2 Mark length required for knicker pattern on inside leg and square across to outside leg, **fig 1.**
3 Square down from crotch line on inside leg, **fig 1.**
4 Reduce at inside leg by 1 cm (⅜ in) from crotch to hem, see broken line, **fig 1.**
5 Lower waist by 1 cm (⅜ in), see broken line, **fig 1.**
6 Measure along crotch curve from point A for 5 cm (2 in). Mark this point C, **fig 2.**
7 Measure along hem line from point B for 5 cm (2 in) mark this D, **fig 2.**
8 Cut away on line from C to D, **fig 3.**
9 Add extra fullness at side seam and waist by marking out at hem by 2 cm (¾ in) and ruling back through hip to waist, see broken line, **fig 3.**
10 Curve leg up by 2 cm (¾ in) over thigh, broken horizontal line, **fig 3.**
11 Trace off for final pattern and mark centre of panel, the grain line should be at 45 degrees from this. Put in balance marks, **fig 4.**
12 If required, the pattern may be shortened slightly at the outside leg hem line, see broken line, **fig 4.**

Back

13 Outline back trouser pattern and square down at inside leg, and square off to outside leg, **fig 5.**
14 Lower back notch line by 1.5 cm (⅝ in), then extend the inside leg down to match the front inside leg pattern and draw a line back to the outside leg seam, **fig 5.**
15 Follow instructions for steps 1-9 as for front pattern, marking in from inside leg E at crotch to points G on curve and F to H on hem, **fig 5.**
16 Cut away crotch on line GH, **fig 6.**
17 At centre of panel on hem line mark down 2 cm (¾ in) and curve back to side seam and CB, **fig 6.**

Gusset

18 Draw a central line 10 cm (4 in) long. This equals the amounts cut from the crotch on back and front patterns. This equals the crotch curve C to G.
19 Measure the length of lines, CD and GH, and mark these out each side of the 10 cm (4 in) line at each end, **fig 7.** Join D to H at both sides of the centre line, **fig 7.**
20 Curve in slightly, see vertical broken lines, **fig 7.**
21 Extend centre line at top and bottom by 5mm to 1 cm (¼ to ⅜ in) and mark out to D and H, **fig 7.**
22 Trace off final pattern, **fig 8.** Cut in fashion fabric with lining in stretch cotton.
23 If a fairly plain, boxer shorts style is wanted, then it is acceptable to join the front and back patterns at the side seam and cut as one with the grain line at 45 degrees from the seam line, **fig 9.**

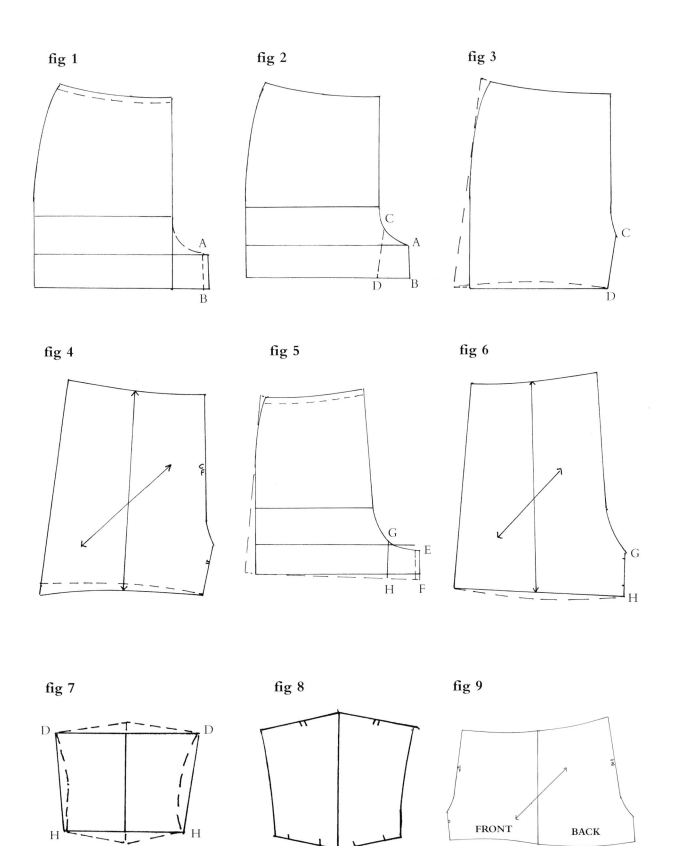

fig 1

fig 2

fig 3

fig 4

fig 5

fig 6

fig 7

fig 8

fig 9

Silk and Lace French Knickers

This design could be cut from either method one or two for French knickers, but it works better when cut from method one. If a plainer garment is wanted, do not divide for lace section, but trim at the hem with narrow lace edging and embroidery.

Front

1 Outline final front pattern from French knickers method one, and mark in centre line, **fig 1.**
2 Slash up line to waist and spread up to 3 cm (1⅛ in), **fig 2.**
3 Trace off and mark in style line for lace seam, put in balance marks, **fig 3.** Mark centre line from waist to hem.
4 Cut away on style line and mark in grain at 45 degrees from centre of panel. Put in balance marks, **fig 4.**
5 Add casing if using elastic waist, see broken line, **fig 4.**
6 Trace off lower front leg and put in grain line at 45 degrees from centre line, **fig 5.** Put in balance marks.

Back

7 Trace off back pattern from method one, **fig 6.**
8 Slash up centre line and spread as for front, **fig 7.**
9 Redraw and mark in style lines, ensuring that front and back marry at the side seam, and cut away as for front, **fig 8.** Grain line 45 degrees on centre of panel.
10 Add casing for elastic.
11 Cut gusset as for French knickers method one.

Waistband

If preferred, a waistband may be used instead of casing. Cut a strip of fashion fabric the same length as the waist of the garment plus a button wrap. Attach around the waist and apply a button and buttonhole. This is the method that would probably have been used in the French knickers of the 1930s.

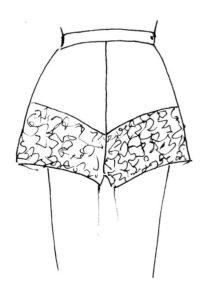

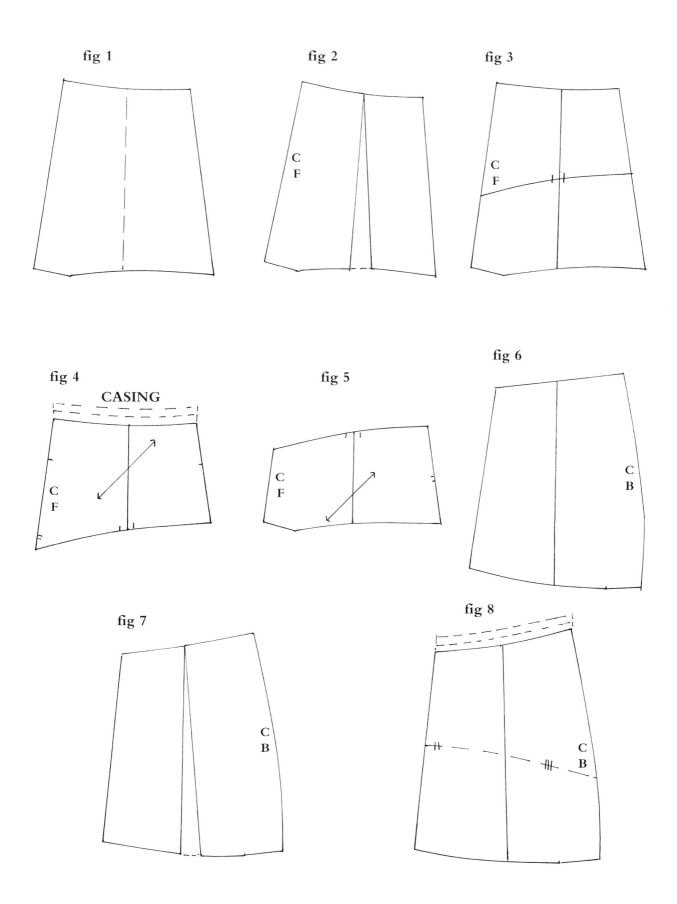

fig 1

fig 2

fig 3

fig 4

CASING

fig 5

fig 6

fig 7

fig 8

Simple French Knickers

A plain design cut from method two, or boxer shorts, pattern.

1 Trace **fig 9** from the boxer shorts pattern and mark in the side seam line, **fig 1.**
2 Divide the front and back sections down the centre at waist and hem, see broken lines, **fig 1.**
3 Slash up these three lines from the hem and spread approximately 3 cm (1⅛ in) each, **fig 2.**
4 Redraw, **fig 3.**
5 Mark in the side seam line down the centre and put in the grain line at 45 degrees from this, **fig 3.**
6 Add casing for elastic as shown in other French knicker patterns.
7 Cut gusset as for French knickers – method two.

This simple and easily made garment is wonderfully comfortable when made in a pure silk satin and either embroidered around the hem or trimmed with fine lace edging.

fig 1

fig 2

fig 3

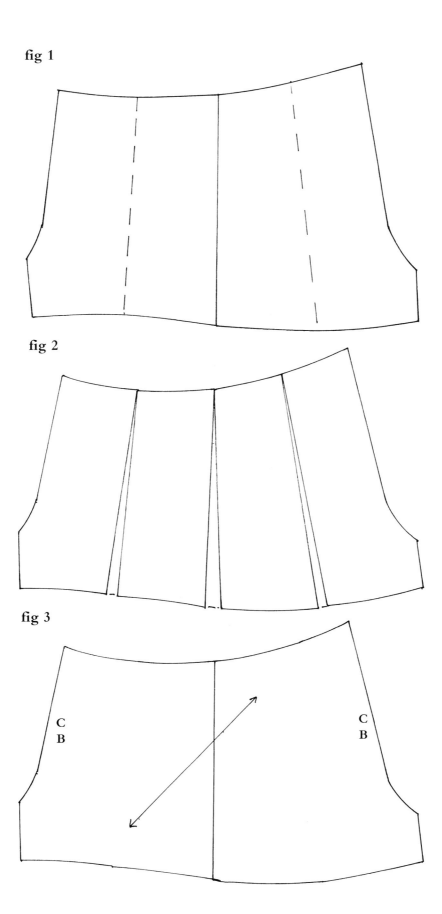

C
B

C
B

Bodies and Camisoles
Straight Top Body with Trim

This simple shape works well for an undergarment or can be worn beneath a jacket or blouse to show at the neck. If preferred, it may be cut with the simple French knicker shape, denoted with broken lines in the diagrams. The trim may be cut in a contrast fabric or lace edging. If contrast fabric is used, then either a bias binding or facing should be used to finish the upper edge of the garment.

Front

1   Outline front body block and mark in style line, dotted line **fig 1.** Put in balance marks.
2   Cut away on style line and place garment pattern with CF on fold of paper, cut and open out to full front, **fig 2.**
3   The small bust dart is used in this style, or the fullness may be eased into the trim if preferred. See the design drawing below.
4   Add the button stand at the crotch, **fig 2.**
5   The waist darts are not used on this style, but if a closer fit is wanted then some extra shaping may be shaved off at the side seam to reflect half the dart.
6   Take the section cut away for the trim and fold out the darts, **fig 3.** Cut with straight grain to CF in lace or on the true bias, if using a woven fabric.

Back

7   Outline block and add style line and balance marks, as for front, **fig 4.**
8   Cut full back pattern, **fig 5.**
9   Ignore the waist darts but shave off half the dart shaping from upper edge to hip, see broken lines, **fig 5.**
10 Extend at the crotch for 10 cm (4 in) and add a button wrap, **fig 5.** Line the gusset with cotton for comfort.
11 For back trim, shave off the dart shaping at the side seams and put in balance marks, **fig 6.**

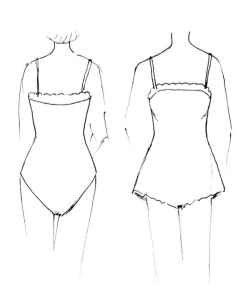

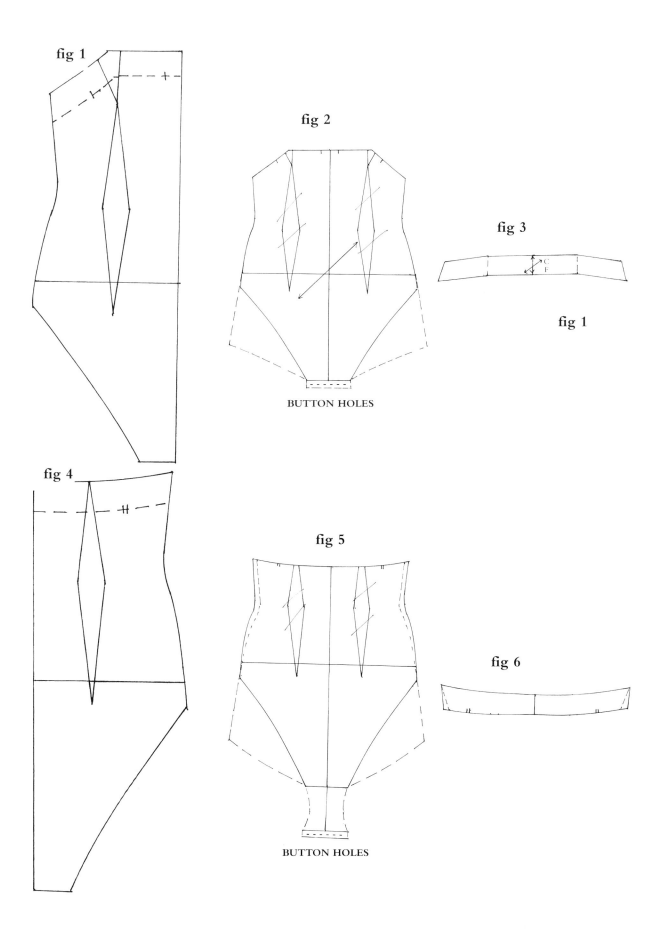

fig 1

fig 2

fig 3

fig 1

BUTTON HOLES

fig 4

fig 5

fig 6

BUTTON HOLES

Classic Body with Seam Shaping

A smooth-fitting garment, this offers a streamlined effect under a fitted garment.

Front

1 Outline front block and draw in bra-style line at upper edge. Ignore waist dart and curve in CF line to reflect some of the dart shaping, **fig 1.**
2 Draw line at right angles from CF to bust point, **fig 1.**
3 Cut away on style lines; cut open line from CF to bust point, and close out the bust dart, **fig 2.** This throws dart shaping on to the CF, it may then be used to gather or pleat for fullness over the bust.
4 Rule across half the width of the pattern at the hip and at the bust and mark vertical line. Grain line should be at 45 degrees from this, **fig 2.** Add button stand at crotch.
5 Cut two.

Back

6 Outline block as for front, and lower the horizontal back line, see broken line, **fig 3.**
7 Ignore the back dart but shave off approximately half the dart at the centre back line, **fig 3.**
8 Redraw pattern, adding a slight curve over the seat, **fig 4.**
9 Cut the gusset as for basic briefs, adding a button wrap. Join to the back at the crotch. Fasten with small plastic poppers.

fig 1

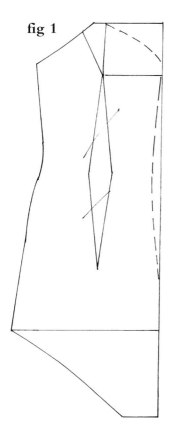

fig 2

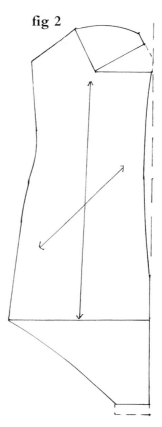

fig 3

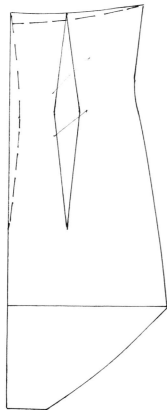

fig 4

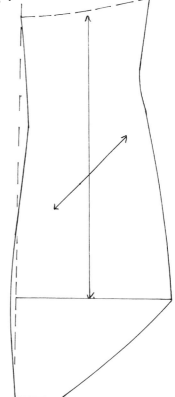

Lace-inset Body

A very glamorous item of lingerie, this is best made in silk satin and fine lace. Lace has a certain amount of give in its construction, and may therefore be cut with the straight grain down the centre of the panel. However, this design is also attractive when made in contrasting woven fabrics. If using woven fabrics, the inset must be cut on the bias.

Front

1   Outline the block and draw in the style lines, see broken lines, **fig 1.** Put in balance marks.
2   Cut away the small bust dart and cut away the inset on the style lines, **fig 2.**
3   Curve in the style line to accommodate some dart shaping, see broken line, **fig 2.**
4   Place CF against fold of paper and cut whole front inset pattern. Soften angle where dart is cut away, see broken lines, **fig 3.**
5   The grain line lies at 45 degrees from CF.
6   On the lower body front, curve off to accommodate some of the dart shaping, see broken lines, **fig 4.**
7   Place CF line to fold of paper and cut full front pattern, **fig 5.** Ensure balance marks are shown. Grain line lies at 45 degrees from CF. Add button stand at crotch.

Back

8   Outline block and draw in style lines, see broken lines, **fig 6.** Put in balance marks.
9   Cut away inset pattern and shape off for dart shaping, **fig 7.**
10   Cut against fold of paper to give full pattern, **fig 8.** The grain line lies at 45 degrees from CB.
11   On lower back pattern, shape in on style line, see broken line, **fig 9.** Place CB on fold of paper and cut whole back as for front, **fig 10.**
12   Draw in the gusset at the back crotch and add button wrap.

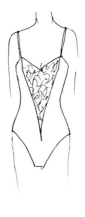

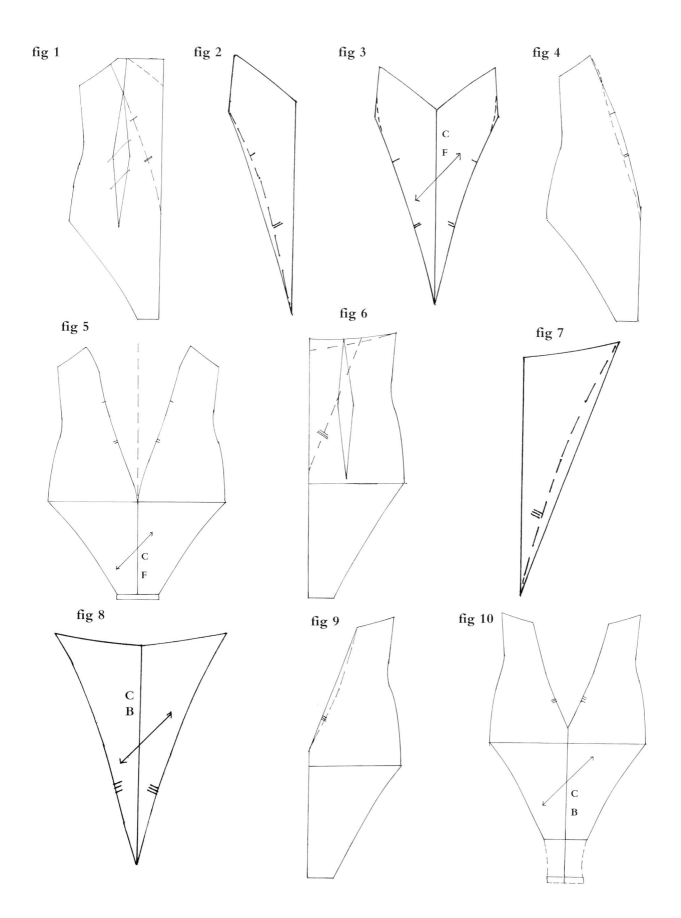

fig 1

fig 2

fig 3

fig 4

fig 5

fig 6

fig 7

fig 8

fig 9

fig 10

Princess-line Body in Silk and Lace

This slender easy-fitting body is best made in luxury fabrics. Lace may be cut with the straight grain through the centre of the panel. If using contrast woven fabrics, the true bias should go through the centre of the panel.

Front

1   Outline the basic body block with the high cut leg and draw in style lines for neck and princess line, **fig 1.** Put in balance marks.
2   With CF on fold of paper, cut away on neckline and cut up from the leg, cutting away all dart shaping, **fig 2.** This gives the seam shaping required for the princess cut.
3   Soften the angle at the waist where the dart has been removed, see broken line, **fig 2.**
4   Open out to whole front pattern and, as lace has natural give, keep grain line to the CF.
5   For the side front panel, trace off and soften the angles made with the removal of darts, see broken line, **fig 3.**
6   Draw a vertical line through the centre of the panel and mark grain at 45 degrees across this, **fig 3.**

Back

7   Outline back block and put in style line from the base of the dart to the leg, see broken line, **fig 4.** Put in balance marks.
8   Cut away on style line and cut away all dart shaping. Place CB on the fold of paper and trace off. Open out and, if using woven fabric, put grain line at 45 degrees from CB, **fig 5.**
9   On side back, draw vertical line through the centre of the panel and mark in grain line at 45 degrees from this, **fig 6.**
10 Follow instructions for the gusset from those for the basic body block.

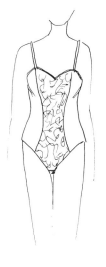
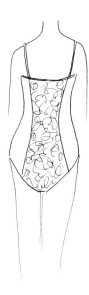

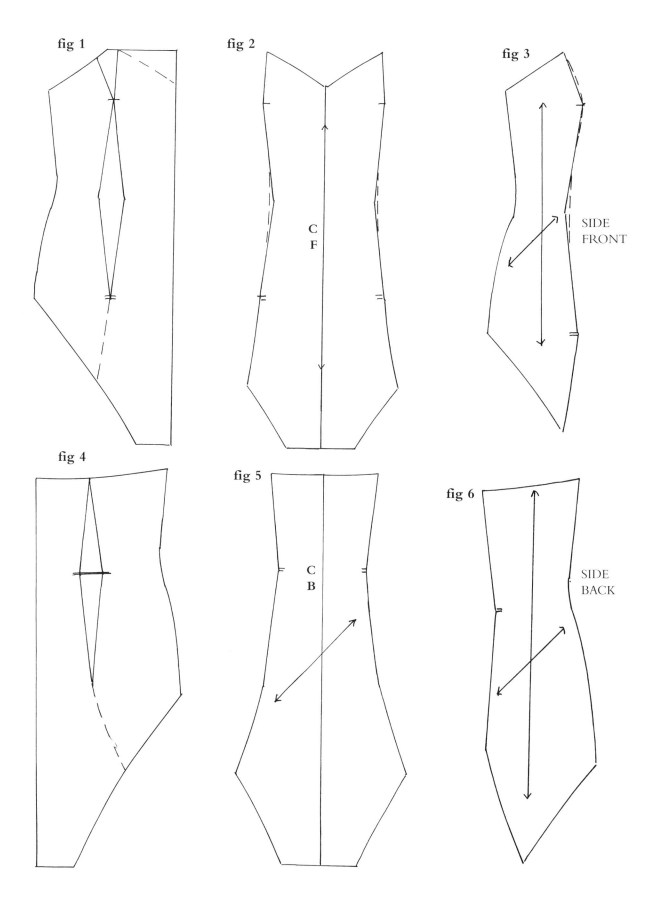

fig 1

fig 2

C F

fig 3

SIDE
FRONT

fig 4

fig 5

C B

fig 6

SIDE
BACK

Lace Petti-top Camiknickers

Pretty as underwear, these are also very effective showing the lace as an evening top to be worn with elegant trousers.

Front

1 Outline the front camiknicker (p. 18) block; dot in the waist dart, and draw in style lines, **fig 1.** Put in balance marks.
2 Cut away on style lines for neckline and waist.
3 On bodice section, slash up through waist dart to bust point and close out the small bust dart from neckline to bust point, thus opening the waist dart, see solid lines, **fig 2.**
4 Measure the width of the dart at the open end and reduce the side seam at the waist by this amount, see broken lines, **fig 2.**
5 Check that the length of the side seam coincides with the original and draw back to CF waist at point, **fig 2.**
6 Trace off, lower the armhole slightly, put in balance marks and the straight grain to CF line, **fig 3.**
7 If using lace, cut one on the fold. If choosing to use a woven contrast fabric, then cut a double pattern and cut fabric singly with true bias at the CF.
8 For the knicker section of the front pattern, ignore the waist dart, shave excess off at side seam if needed to fit with the bodice, see broken line, **fig 4.** Mark grain line at 45 degrees from CF.

Back

9 Trace off the back block and draw in the style lines, see broken lines, **fig 5.** Put in balance marks.
10 Ignore the dart but shave a little off the side seam to compensate, see broken vertical line, **fig 5.**
11 Cut away on the style lines and on the bodice mark the straight grain to the CB fold; alternatively, if using a contrast woven fabric instead of lace, show the true bias on the CB, **fig 6.**
12 On the back knicker section, mark in the true bias on the CB line, **fig 7.** Put in balance marks.
13 Cut the gusset as in the basic camiknicker block and finish either open with fastening or attached to both the back and front garment.

If the lace used does not have sufficient natural stretch then it may be necessary to insert a zip or placket in the side of the garment.

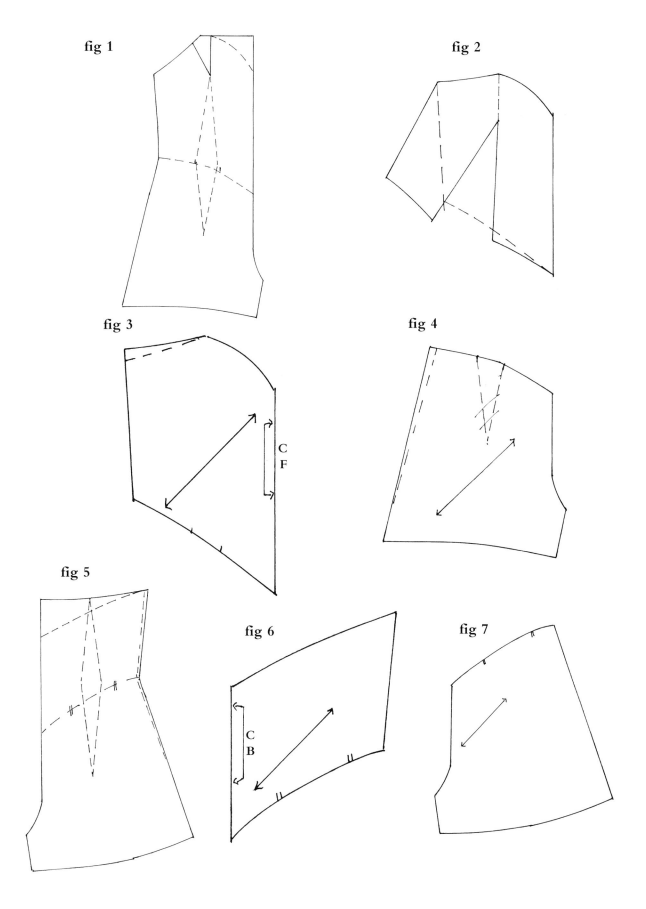

fig 1

fig 2

fig 3

fig 4

fig 5

fig 6

fig 7

C F

C B

Princess-line Camiknickers

This garment may be made with a contrasting trim around the upper edge, perhaps using plain and jacquard fabrics in the same colour. Alternatively the trim could be cut in lace.

Front

1   Outline camiknicker block and draw in style line for trim. Narrow waist dart to about half the original size at waist and angle off to centre of leg, see broken lines, **fig 1.** Put in balance marks.
2   Cut away trim and fold out bust dart, **fig 2.**
3   Place CF on fold of paper and cut out full pattern for trim, **fig 2.** Mark grain at 45 degrees from CF line.
4   Trace off the CF section of front body to revised dart line, cutting away the dart, **fig 3.**
5   Put in balance marks and draw a vertical line through the centre of the panel, **fig 3.** The grain line is at 45 degrees off the CF line.
6   Trace off side front panel to revised dart line, cutting away dart. Put in balance marks and mark centre of panel. The grain line lies at 45 degrees from this, **fig 4.**

Back

7   Trace off back camiknicker block and draw in style lines, see broken line, **fig 5.** Ignore dart on trim section but reduce side seam by the same amount, see broken line at side seam, **fig 5.**
8   Reduce waist dart by half and angle from waist to centre of leg at hem, see broken vertical lines, **fig 5.**
9   Cut away trim section and trace off with CB line against fold of paper, then open to whole width of back pattern. The grain line lies at 45 degrees from CB line, **fig 6.**
10 Trace off CB pattern to the waist dart, cutting away shaping as for the front pattern. Draw a vertical line through the centre of the panel and mark the true bias (45 degrees) from this line, **fig 7**.
11 Trace off the side back section to the revised dart shaping, and mark grain line as for CB panel. Put in balance marks, **fig 8**.
12 Cut and make gusset as for basic camiknicker block pattern.

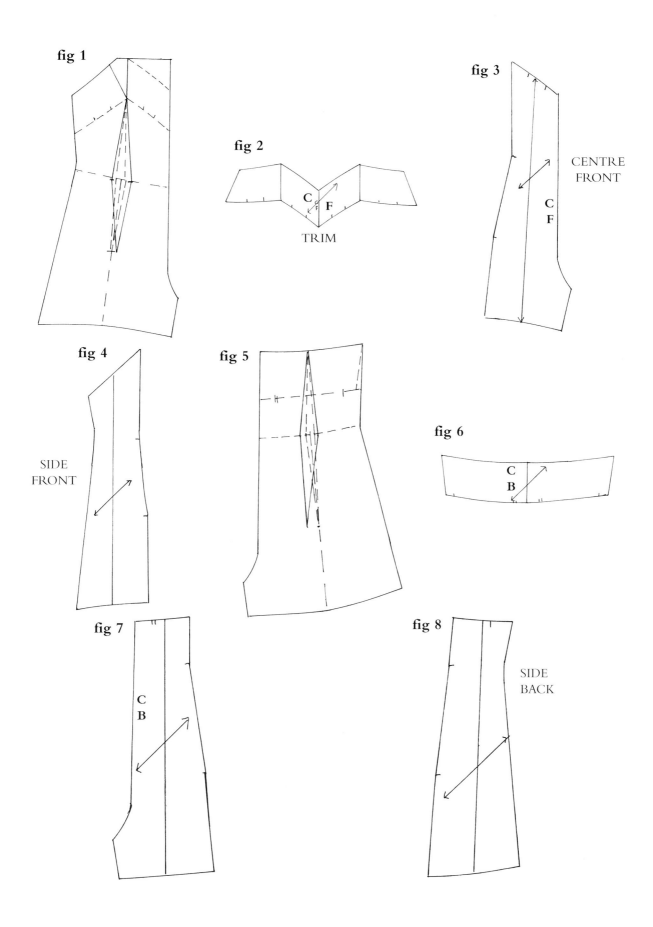

fig 1

fig 2

C
F

TRIM

fig 3

CENTRE
FRONT

C
F

fig 4

SIDE
FRONT

fig 5

fig 6

C
B

fig 7

C
B

fig 8

SIDE
BACK

Bra-top Camiknickers

For this garment, the bra must be cut double and bagged out. A channel is then stitched on the under bust seam and underwiring inserted. Across the void between the bra cups a piece of decorative elastic should be applied, alternatively a casing may be made and elastic threaded through. This prevents the cups from parting company.

Front

1   Outline the camiknicker block and draw in the bust style line, see broken lines, **fig 1.** Put in balance marks.
2   Cut away on the style lines and cut vertically through the bra section, cutting away the bust dart to leave two separate pieces, **fig 2.**
3   Soften the angle at the bust point, **fig.2.**
4   Mark in the grain lines at 45 degrees from the bust point, **fig 2.**
5   On the front body section, mark the centre of the panel at underbust line and hem. Draw a line through this, see broken line, **fig 3.**
6   Slash up the vertical line to the waist, opening the leg, and fold out the dart to the top of the pattern piece, **fig 4.**
7   Reduce the underbust curve towards the CF, thereby shortening the angled line to the seam, see broken line, **fig 4.**
8   Trace off final pattern and put in balance marks, **fig 5.**

Back

9   Outline the block and draw in back style line, see broken line, **fig 6.**
10   Cut away on style line, **fig 7.**
11   Ignore the waist dart, but reduce at side seam by a similar amount to the top of the dart, see broken vertical line at side seam, **fig 7.**
12   The style line will now gape unless it is shortened. Draw in a line from the style line to the centre of the dart shaping and then angle down to the centre of the leg at the hem, see broken lines, **fig 7.**
13   Slash up this line to the waist and then pinch out a small dart shaped area of the pattern from the style line, **fig 8.**
14   Trace off the final pattern and put in balance marks.
15   Draw in line down the centre of the panel and mark true bias (45 degrees) from this, **fig 9**.
16   To make the gusset , follow the instructions for the basic camiknicker block.

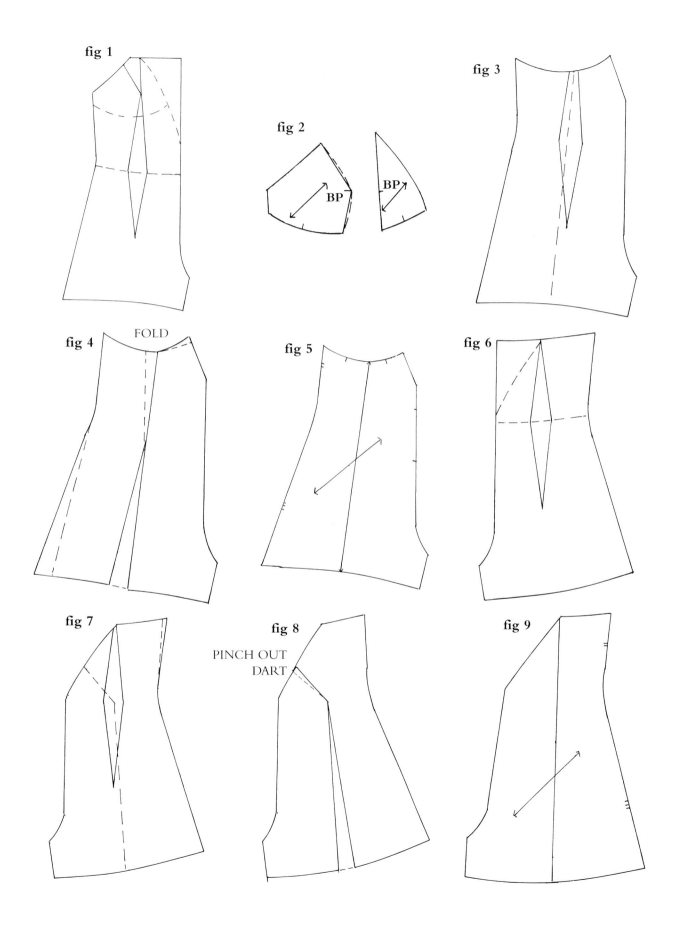

fig 1

fig 2

fig 3

fig 4

FOLD

fig 5

fig 6

fig 7

fig 8

PINCH OUT
DART

fig 9

Lace-edged Camisole

For all camisole patterns, use the lingerie block shortened to the camisole line (top hip line). This is a basic shape for a camisole top that fits smoothly under most blouses or sweaters.

Front

1   Outline block to hip and shorten to camisole line. Ignore waist dart. Draw in style line from CF to bust dart and soften waist curve, see broken lines, **fig 1.**
2   Trace off and draw in style line for lace edging, and put in balance marks, **fig 2.**
3   Cut away trim sections and draw the front pattern with CF to fold; open out to whole front, use bust dart for easing into lace trim, see broken line, **fig 3.** Put in grain line at 45 degrees to CF line.
4   Use ready-made double-edged lace of the appropriate width for trim, mitring at corners over the bust shaping and underarm and at the corner at the lower edge.

Back

5   Outline block as for front and cut away depth required for top and bottom trim, **fig 4.**
6   Attach trim as for front, mitring at corners.

When stitching the lace to the garment, it is best to use a zigzag stitch over the edge of the trim, as this allows some 'give' when putting the camisole over the head.

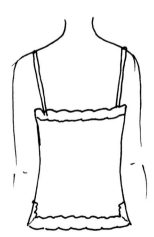

fig 1

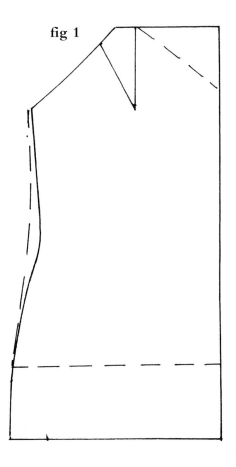

fig 2

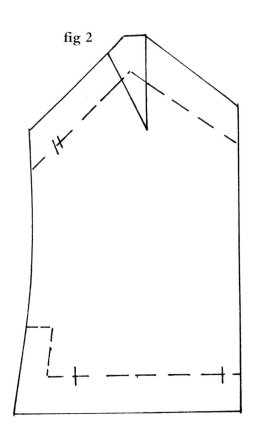

fig 3

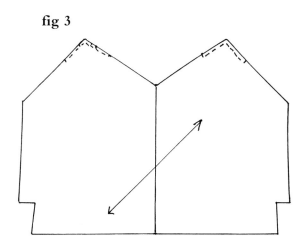

fig 4

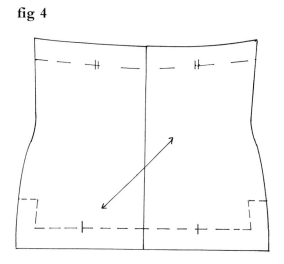

Scoop-neck Camisole with Bound Edges

A very simple and easy-to-wear camisole, this looks good under a low-cut jacket. This design also makes an attractive easy-fitting sun top.

Front

1   Outline lingerie block to camisole line and soften side seam at waist, see broken line, **fig 1.**
2   Draw a line at a right angle to CF up to bust point of dart and curve off neckline from top of dart to CF line, see broken lines, **fig 1.** Curve hem, **fig 1.**
3   Trace off; slash open line from CF to bust point, and close dart, **fig 2.** Square off CF line.
4   Place CF line against fold of pattern paper and redraw, open out to whole front. Mark in gathering lines each side of CF to a depth of about 8 cm (3 in), **fig 3.**
5   Draw in grain line at 45 degrees to CF line, **fig 3.**

Back

6   Outline block and curve off upper edge from armhole to CB, **fig 4.**
7   Soften waist shaping and draw in hem line to match that of front pattern, **fig 4.**
8   Trace off against fold of paper and put in grain line as for front, **fig 5.**

Bind the edges with bias strips cut from fashion fabric and make rouleau straps for shoulders.

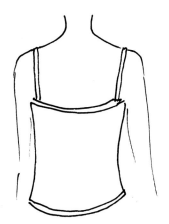

fig 1

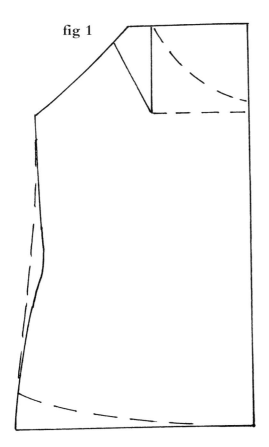

fig 2

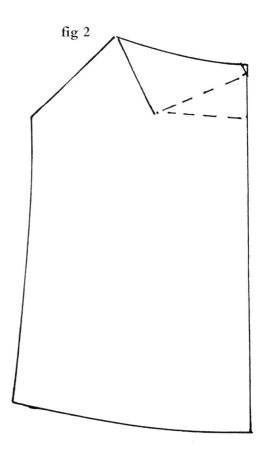

fig 3

fig 4

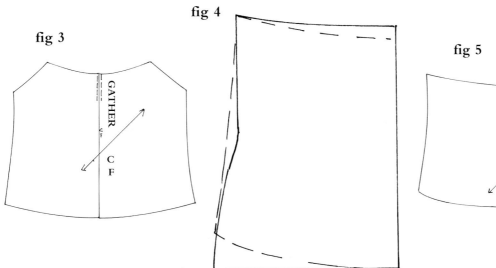

GATHER

C
F

fig 5

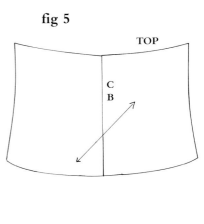

TOP

C
B

Lace Bib Camisole

This is an attractive design, which may be worn with the bib showing at the neck of a blouse or jacket.

Front

1   Outline lingerie block to camisole line and soften the curve at the waist on the side seam. Ignore waist darts, see broken line, **fig 1.**

2   Draw in the style line from the point of the bust dart to required depth on CF line, see broken line, **fig 1.** Put in balance marks. Cut away bib section on style line. Remove dart.

3   Trace front with CF line on fold of paper, open out to whole front, put in balance marks, with the grain line at 45 degrees to CF, **fig 2.**

4   Trace off bib section on folded paper, open out as above, and put in balance marks, **fig 3.**

5   If you are using lace, this may be cut with the straight grain to CF line, as there is some stretch in all lace. If using a contrast colour or texture woven fabric for the bib – for example, a jacquard bib with plain bodice – this should be cut on the true bias, 45 degrees from the CF, **fig 3.**

Back

6   Outline the block, softening the waist curve as for front, see broken line, **fig 4.**

7   Raise the upper edge to a point above the dart line and curve back to CB and underarm, see broken lines, **fig 4.**

Use rouleau, cut from fashion fabric or ribbon, to make straps.

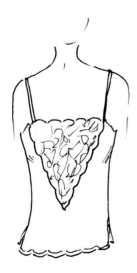

fig 1

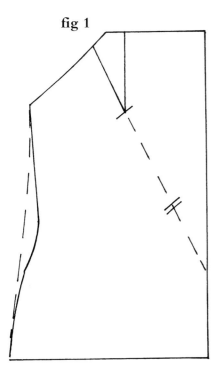

fig 2

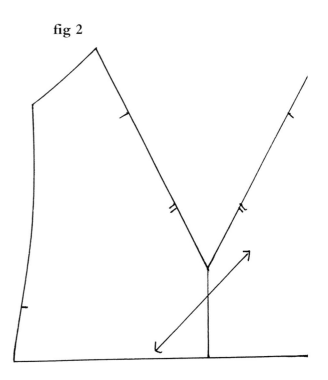

fig 3

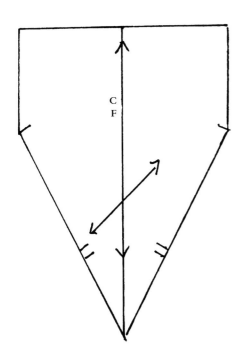

fig 4

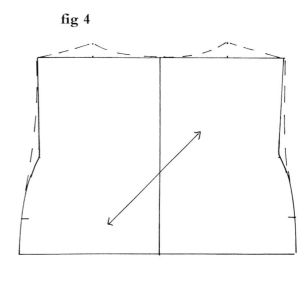

Tucked Princess Camisole

An elegant style, this may be used either for underwear or for a simple top to be worn under a jacket.

Front

1   Cut from the fitted garment pattern *before* cutting away the shoulder section for lingerie. Trace off to the camisole line, **fig 1.** Include the waist darts. Soften the waist curve at side seam, see broken line, **fig 1.** Trace the lingerie line at right angles to CF, but continue the outer edge of the dart up to the shoulder and including the armhole, **fig 1.**
2   Draw in the armhole for the design, see broken line, **fig 1**, and put in balance marks.
3   Cut away side front pattern from CF pattern, cutting out around the dart shaping, **fig 2.** This gives a curved seam to accommodate the bust shape. Soften the angles at bust and waist, see broken lines, **fig 2.**
4   Mark dart across strap from armhole and fold to shorten inner edge, thus shortening the neck edge of the strap, **fig 3.**
5   Trace off and mark centre of panel, grain line at 45 degrees from this, **fig 3.**
6   Trace off CF panel against fold of paper and open out to whole. Soften angles, see broken lines, **fig 4**, and put in balance marks.

7   Mark in position of tucks, see broken lines, **fig 4.** Slash across these lines and lengthen pattern by depth required for tuck.

Back

8   Trace off the lingerie block to camisole line as for front, **fig 5.** Soften waist curve.
9   Draw in strap line from top of waist dart to shoulder and draw in new armhole, see broken lines, **fig 5.** Take care to match width of strap from back to front patterns.
10 Trace off CB panel to folded paper and open out; mark in tuck lines and lengthen pattern accordingly, **fig 6.** Put in balance marks.
11 For side back, trace off cut away section and soften waist curve, **fig 7.** Mark in dart shape across strap as for front, **fig 7.**
12 Fold out dart at inner (neck) edge, thus straightening the line of the strap, **fig 8.**
13 Mark centre of panel, **fig 8.**
14 Trace off final pattern and draw in grain line at 45 degrees to vertical line.

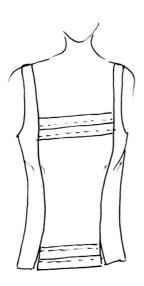

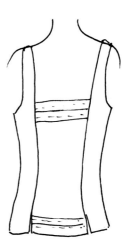

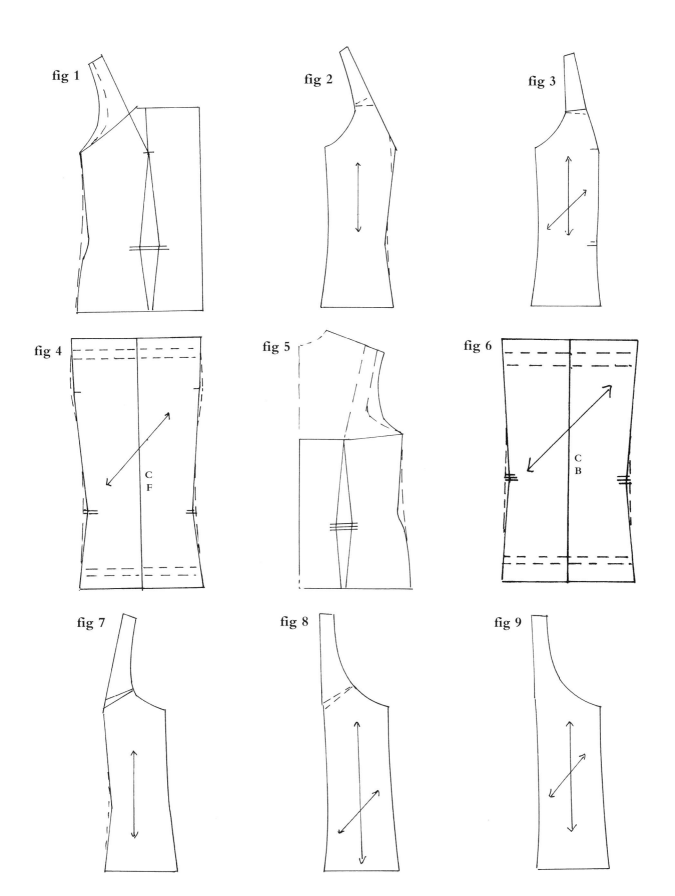

Bustier

This is only suitable for a fairly small busted figure, young enough for gravity not to have taken its toll!

Front

1 Outline the lingerie block including the shoulder section, **fig 1.**
2 Draw in the style line for neck and under-bust line, see broken lines, **fig 2.**
3 Cut away on style lines and up inner edge of shoulder dart, **fig 3.**
4 Slash open under bust dart to point and close out shoulder dart, **fig 4.**
5 From point of dart to neck edge, pinch out a small dart in the pattern, thus shortening the neck length and opening the under-bust dart further, **fig 5.** Straighten shoulder, see broken line, **fig 5.**
6 Trace off pattern and add button wrap and facing to CF line, **fig 6.** Put in grain line at 45 degrees from CF.

Back

7 Outline block as for front and draw in neck and under-bust style lines, see broken lines, **fig 7.** Take care to match to front at side seam.
8 Cut away on style line, draw a line from the dart point to neckline. Straighten the shoulder, see broken line, **fig 8.**
9 Slash open the dart and pinch a dart into the pattern at neck edge along the line, **fig 9.**
10 Measure the width of the dart at the base and shave off this amount at the side seam, taking off to nothing at underarm, **fig 9**. If necessary, adjust side seam to match front side seam.
11 Trace off with CB to fold of paper and open out, put grain line in at 45 degrees from CB line, **fig 10.**
12 Add casing at the hem and thread elastic through. Bind and trim neck and armhole edges.

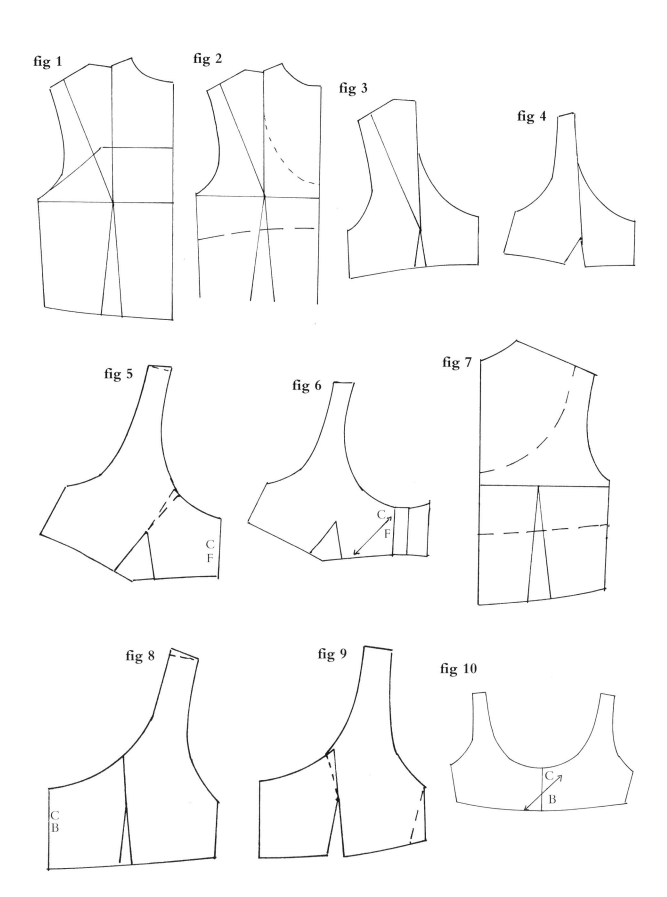

fig 1

fig 2

fig 3

fig 4

fig 5

fig 6

fig 7

fig 8

fig 9

fig 10

Skirts and Waist Slips

Gently Flared Bias Skirt

This is a basic shape for a bias-cut skirt, which can be adjusted to any length. It is wise to use a side seam zip to avoid breaking up the line at CB.

Front

1. Outline the block over whole front (left and right), and lengthen or shorten as needed. Draw vertical lines to dart points (darts will be removed), **fig 1.**
2. Slash up vertical lines to base of each dart and close darts out, thereby opening pattern at hem, **fig 2.**
3. Reduce curve at hip, see broken vertical line, **fig 2.**
4. Soften angles at waist, see broken horizontal line, **fig 2.**
5. Trace off pattern and draw grain line at 45 degrees from CF line, **fig 3.** Put in balance marks.

Back

6. Outline block over whole back and follow instructions for steps 1–5, as for front.

It is sometimes better to insert a zip by hand in a bias-cut garment as it is easier to prevent stretch or pucker this way.

Always test stitch a bias seam on the fashion fabric before working on the garment. If need be you can reduce foot pressure to prevent stretching, and it may be wise to use a very small zigzag stitch, which will allow the fabric to drop slightly.

Before adjusting the hem, hang the garment for about seven days to allow the fabric to drop. After hemming, store the garment flat when it is not being worn.

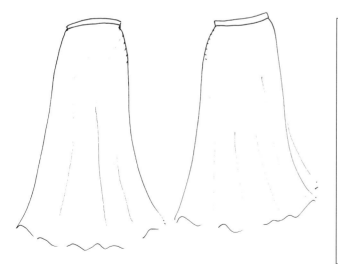

NOTE
This and most of the other skirts in the book may be cut from any basic straight skirt block or the lingerie block may be traced off from waist to hem and the size of the darts both back and front increased to create a snug fit at the waist.

Waistbands should be cut to the length of the garment waist, *not* to the wearer's waist. Measure the garment and add the button stand. Cut twice the finished depth of waistband and seam allowances.

fig 1

fig 2

fig 3

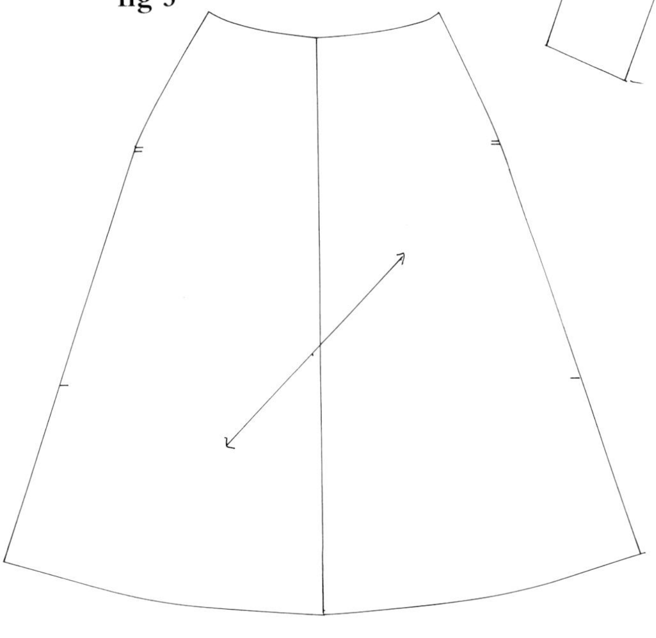

Semi-straight Bias Skirt

The semi-straight skirt is a simple bias shape, which may be cut to any length and can look good with a straight-cut frill at the hem.

Front

1 Outline front block to required length, **fig 1.**
2 Delete the darts and curve in at hips to equal half the dart width, see broken line, **fig 1.**
3 Raise the waist at side seam, continuing hip curve, **fig 1.**
4 Widen slightly at the side seam hem, say 4 to 5 cm (1½ to 2 in) and draw back to hip, see broken line, **fig 1.**
5 Curve down slightly to CF at hem, **fig 1.**
6 Trace off and draw in grain line at 45 degrees from CF line, **fig 2.** Put in balance marks.

Back

7 Using back block follow instructions for steps 1–6, as for front.

Frill

8 Measure the circumference of the hem and cut a straight strip twice this length with straight grain to CF. Gather evenly and stitch to hem of skirt.

If necessary ease the skirt on to the waistband. Otherwise cut lining as above and join to skirt at waist with tape to prevent stretch, which means no waistband is needed

fig 1

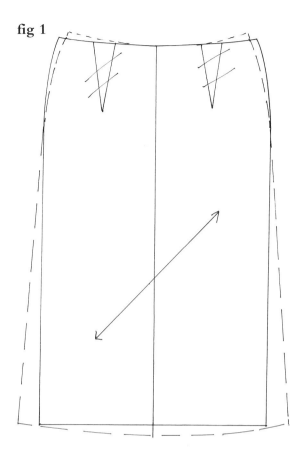

fig 2

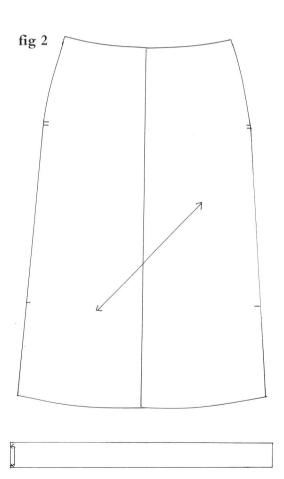

Skirt with Asymmetric Flounce

A very glamorous garment, this stylish skirt is cut slim over the hips but with lots of movement in the flounce. Each pattern piece is cut singly.

Front

1 Working from basic skirt block (not from lingerie block), outline whole front block. Lengthen as required and draw in flounce style line, broken line **fig 1.** Put in balance marks.
2 Cut away on style line and put in straight grain down CF line, **fig 2.**
3 Divide flounce into six equal sections, **fig 3.** Slash and spread equally each side of CF line, **fig 4.** It is worth noting that spreading should be generous, otherwise the finished garment can look skimpy.
4 Trace off and put grain line at 45 degrees to CF line, **fig 5**.

Back

5 Match flounce style line at side seams with the front pattern.
6 Follow instructions above for steps 1-4, but ensure that balance marks for back patterns are in a different position from those on the front. The flounce should be spread the same amount as for front.

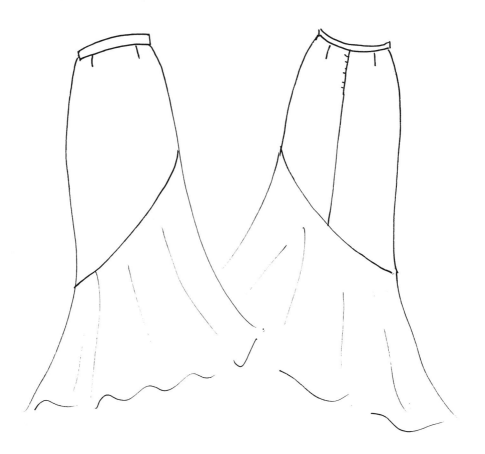

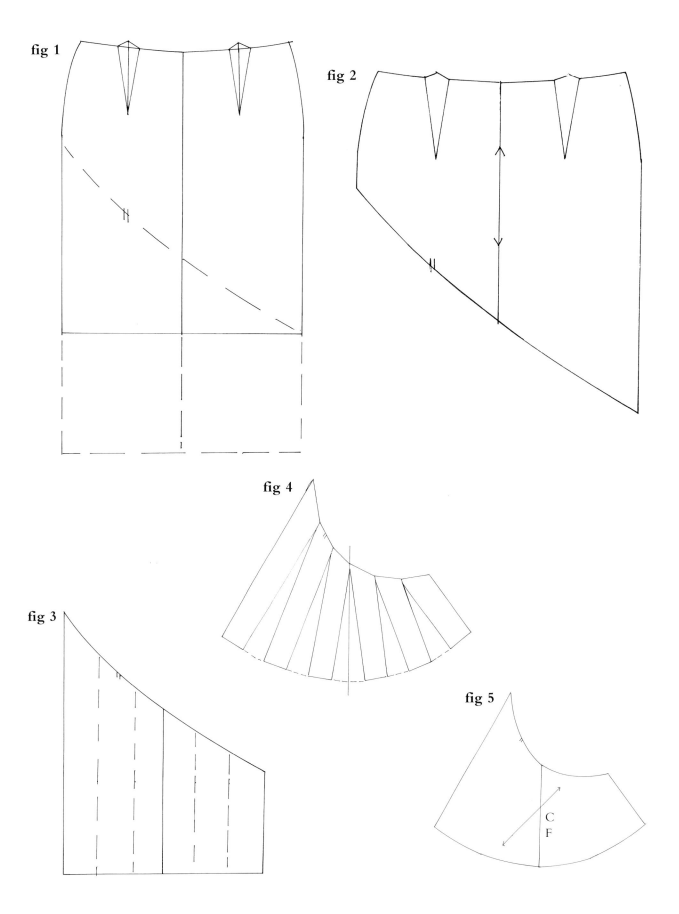

fig 1

fig 2

fig 4

fig 3

fig 5

C
F

Layered Mini-skirt

This skirt is eternally popular with the young. It is cut as two circular skirts, one longer than the other and joined together into the waistband. It may be cut with several layers if desired and could be equally attractive in a longer style.

Front and Back

1 Take the waist measurement and add 2.5 cm (1 in) ease. To find the radius of the waist, divide by 6.3: for example, for a standard size 12, waist 66 cm + 2.5 cm = 68.5 cm (26 in + 1 in = 27 in) divide by 6.3 = 10.8 cm (4⅓ in).

2 Mark a central vertical line on pattern paper and draw a horizontal extending 10.8 cm (4⅓ in) at each side, mark the same measurement around a half circle, see broken line, **fig 1.**

3 The half circle is now half the waist measurement. Draw the desired length of the skirt on to this, see solid outline, **fig 1.**

4 Mark grain line at 45 degrees to the centre line, **fig 2.** Cut two.

Underlayer

5 Follow instructions as above, cutting the skirt approx. 12 to 15 cm (5 to 6 in) longer than the outer layer.

When cutting the fabric, add seam allowances where applicable, and around the waist machine stitch on the fitting line. Clip through the seam allowance to the stitching/fitting line at intervals along this edge, **fig 3.** This allows the fabric to straighten out without tearing, for waistband application.

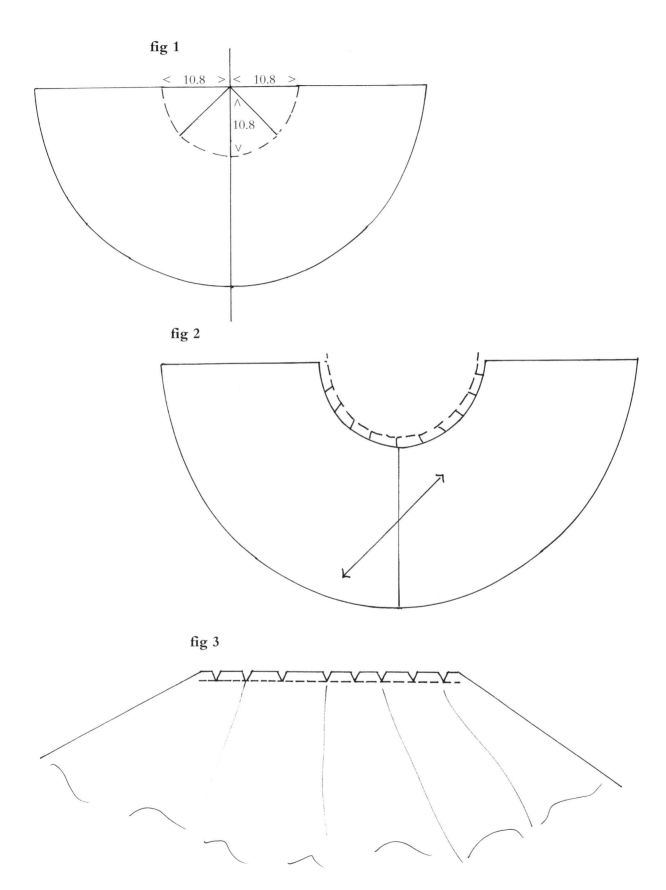

fig 1

fig 2

fig 3

Handkerchief-point Layered Skirt

This wonderfully elegant skirt is also cut on a circular construction. It is lovely when made in softly draping crepe or in contrasting fabrics; for example, a crepe layer topped with chiffon.

Front and Back

1   Take the waist measurement and add 2.5 cm (1 in) ease. To find the radius of the waist, divide by 6.3: for example, for a standard size 12, waist 66 cm + 2.5 cm = 68.5 cm (26 in + 1 in = 27 in) divide by 6.3 = 10.8 cm (4⅓ in).

2   Mark a centre vertical line on pattern paper and draw a horizontal line extending 10.8 cm (4⅓ in) at each side. Mark the same measurement around a half circle, see broken line, **fig 1.**

3   The half circle is now half the waist measurement. Draw the desired length of the skirt on to this, see solid outline, **fig 1.** Square off for corners. When cutting the garment this is cut on the fold of fabric, **fig 1.**

4   Cut both squares of fabric and place one over the other pivoting round as shown in **fig 2.**

5   Mark the waist radius on the centre of the panel and scoop out, making sure enough fabric is left for the seam allowance.

6   Decide where the zipper seam should be and mark a straight line from hem to waist. Cut open, see broken horizontal line, **fig 2.**

When making the garment up, stay stitch around the waist line and clip open; join the seam, and insert the zip. Ensure the waist measurement is accurate, and apply the skirt to the waistband.

fig 1

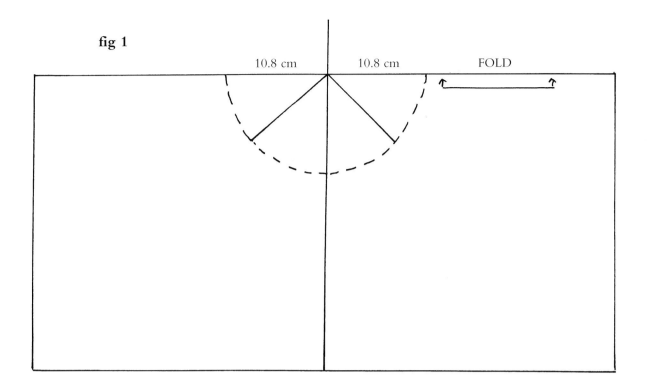

10.8 cm   10.8 cm   FOLD

fig 2

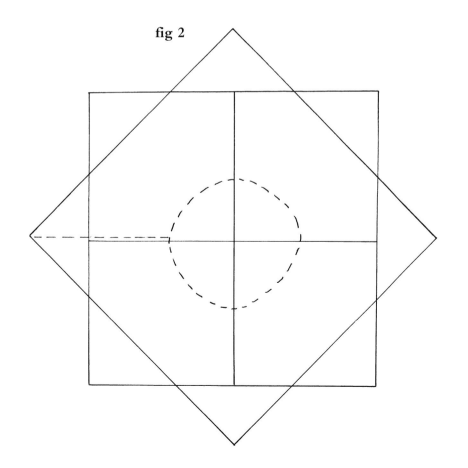

Yoked Waist Slip

A versatile slip pattern, this creates a slip that is slim over the tummy but gives fullness at the hem. You could use it for a simple skirt, provided the pattern is given some waist shaping and a waistband.

Front and Back

1 Outline front and back blocks (lingerie or skirt) excluding dart shaping. Lengthen or shorten as appropriate.
2 Draw in yoke style line and put in balance mark. Square off at waist and side seam, see broken lines, **fig 1.** Cut away yoke.
3 On skirt, divide vertically into equal sections, **fig 2.**
4 Slash through these lines and spread for fullness, **fig 3.** This may be spread any amount up to a quarter circle. Dot in to join sections, **fig 3.**
5 Trace off with fold of pattern paper to CF line, open out and draw grain line at 45 degrees off CF, **fig 4.**
6 For yoke, trace off on fold of paper as above; add casing for elastic, and draw in grain line as above, **fig 5.**

A lace trim should be applied at hem and yoke line.

fig 1

fig 2

fig 4

fig 3

fig 5

CASING

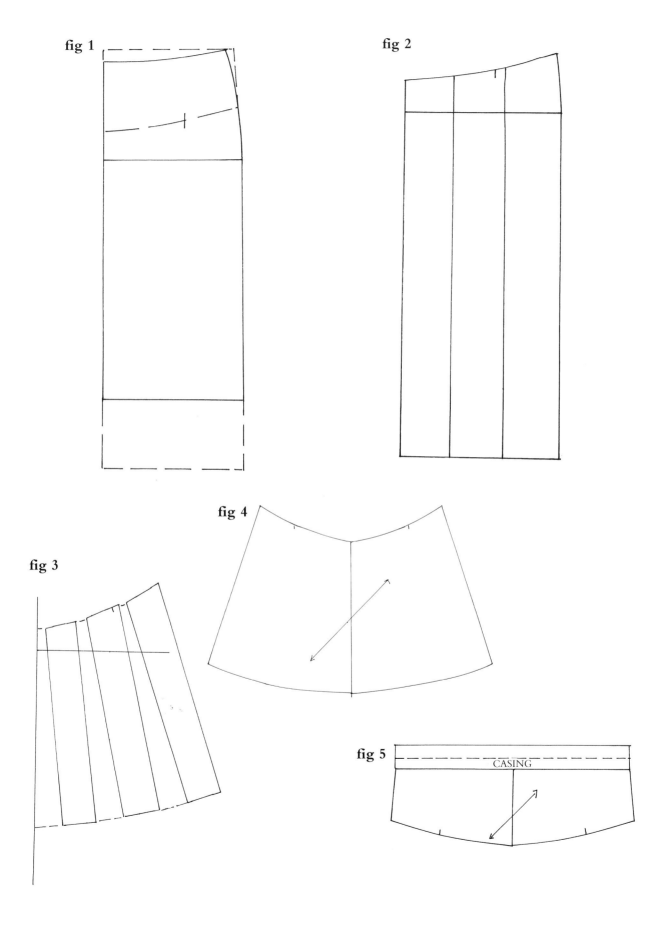

Petal-fronted Waist Slip

This is a simple slip with minimal bulk, designed to fit smoothly under a straight skirt.

Front

1 Outline front lingerie or skirt block, ignoring waist darts, see solid lines, **fig 1.**
2 Allow a small amount of stride room at side seam hem and rule back to nothing at hip, see broken line, **fig 1.**
3 Continue this line to waist level and square off to CF line, see broken lines, **fig 1.**
4 Draw in curve at CF hem, **fig 1.**
5 Divide in half at hip and half at original block hem and draw a vertical line, **fig 1.**
6 Trace off final pattern and add casing for waist elastic, **fig 2.**
7 Draw grain line at 45 degrees to the vertical centre of original block shape.

Back

8 Outline whole back lingerie or skirt block, ignoring waist darts.
9 Follow steps 2-7 as for front, **fig 3.**
10 Add casing at waist.

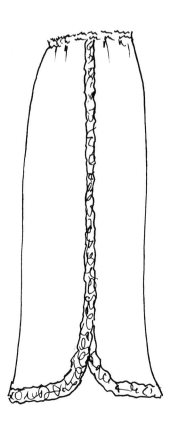

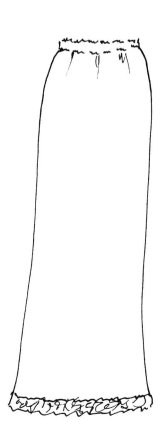

fig 1

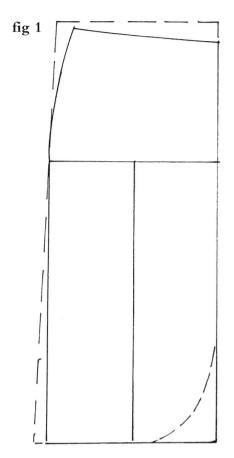

fig 2

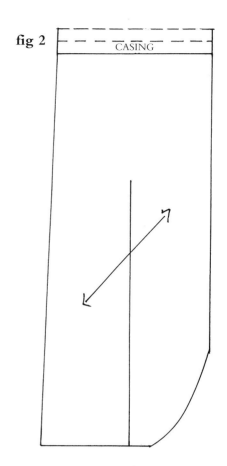

fig 3

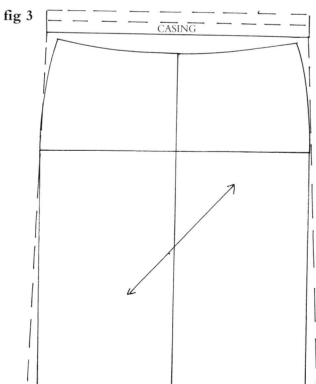

Four-gore Waist Slip

This garment may be made with or without a frill at the hem. Without the frill it should have a lace or embroidered trim at the hem. The shape skims the hips while allowing fullness under a shaped skirt.

Front and back

1 Outline blocks (lingerie or skirt) and square off at waist. Lengthen as needed, see broken lines, **fig 1.** Draw in vertical centre line from hip to hem.
2 This may also be taken from direct measurements: take hip measurement plus ease; divide by four, and draw a rectangle the width of quarter-hip by the length required, **fig 2.**
3 Divide rectangle pattern into equal sections, **fig 2.**
4 Slash up all lines but not through at waist and spread evenly from the centre, **fig 3.**
5 Trace off final pattern including centre vertical line and draw in grain line at 45 degrees from this, **fig 4.**

Frill

6 Shorten the main pattern to allow for depth of frill.
7 Cut a straight piece of fabric approximately twice the length of the circumference of the garment at hem.
8 Run two parallel lines of loose machine stitching along one edge and pull up to fit the hem of the garment, **fig 5.**
9 Machine to hem and trim as desired.

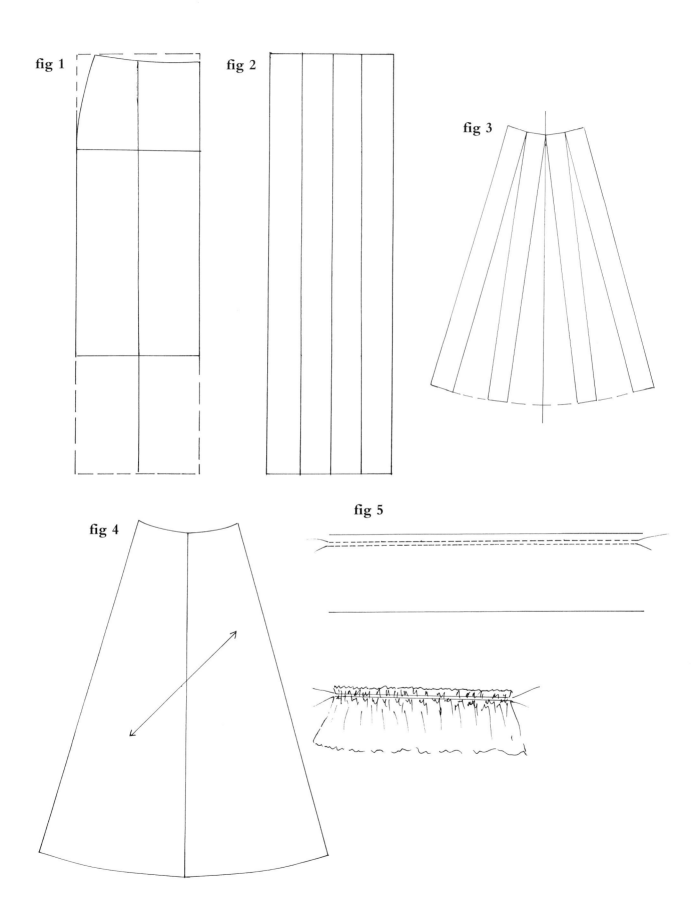

fig 1

fig 2

fig 3

fig 4

fig 5

Trousers

Bias Culottes

This garment may be cut to any length and is equally attractive at knee, calf and floor length.

Front

1 Outline straight skirt block and delete the dart, **fig 1.** Lengthen or shorten as needed.
2 Measure down from the waist to crotch depth and draw in crotch line parallel with hip and approximately 10 cm (4 in) down, **fig 1.**
3 Extend this line at the CF by a quarter of the hip line, **fig 1,** and draw inside leg line parallel with CF.
4 From hip to crotch line curve off to nothing at each point, see broken line, **fig 1.**
5 Curve in from hip to waist by half the dart measurement and raise waist by approximately 1 cm (⅜ in) at side seam. Curve back to waistline, see broken lines, **fig 2.**
6 At CF waist mark in 1 to 1½ cm (⅝ to ¾ in) and draw back to nothing at hip, **fig 2.**

7 At hem, widen equally at outside and inside leg and rule back to nothing at hip and crotch, broken line **fig 2.**
8 Trace off and mark centre of crotch and centre of hem, draw straight line from point to point and mark in grain line at 45 degrees from this, **fig 3.**
9 Curve off slightly at hem, see broken line, **fig 3.**

Back

10 Follow steps 1-9 as for front pattern. Put in balance marks at hip level on front and back patterns.

fig 1

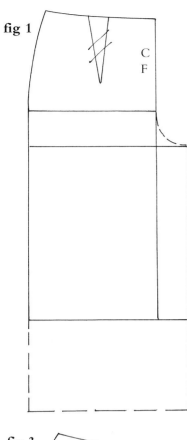

C
F

fig 2

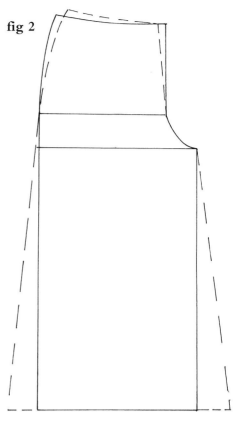

fig 3

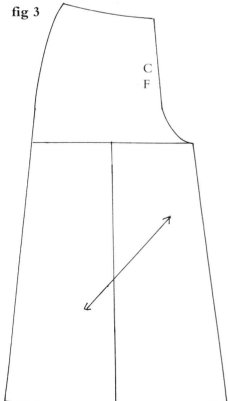

C
F

fig 4

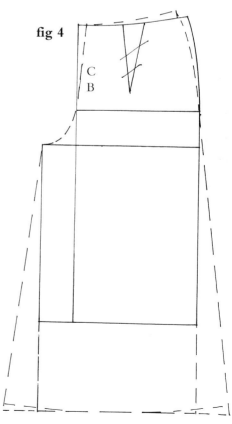

C
B

Palazzo Pants

An elegant 1930s style, these pants are suitable for evening wear or for very glamorous pyjamas. They look good with a simple kimöno-cut jacket.

Front and back

1 Follow instructions for basic pattern from Bias culottes (previous page), **figs 1-2.**
2 Join front and back together from hip to hem, **fig 3.** This forms a natural dart at the side waist.
3 Draw vertical line from the point of darts to the hem on back and front, **fig 3.**
4 Slash up these lines to dart point on front, back and side and fold out darts, thereby spreading lines for flare. Ensure spreading is equal at either side of centre line, **fig 4.**

5 Soften the angles at waistline and join the slashed sections at hem, see broken lines, **fig 4.**
6 Trace outline pattern, including centre line, and draw in grain line at 45 degrees to this. Apart from the waistband, there is only the one pattern piece for this garment, cut 2.

Because of the length and considerable fullness of the design it may be necessary to join two pieces of fabric in order to achieve the width needed.

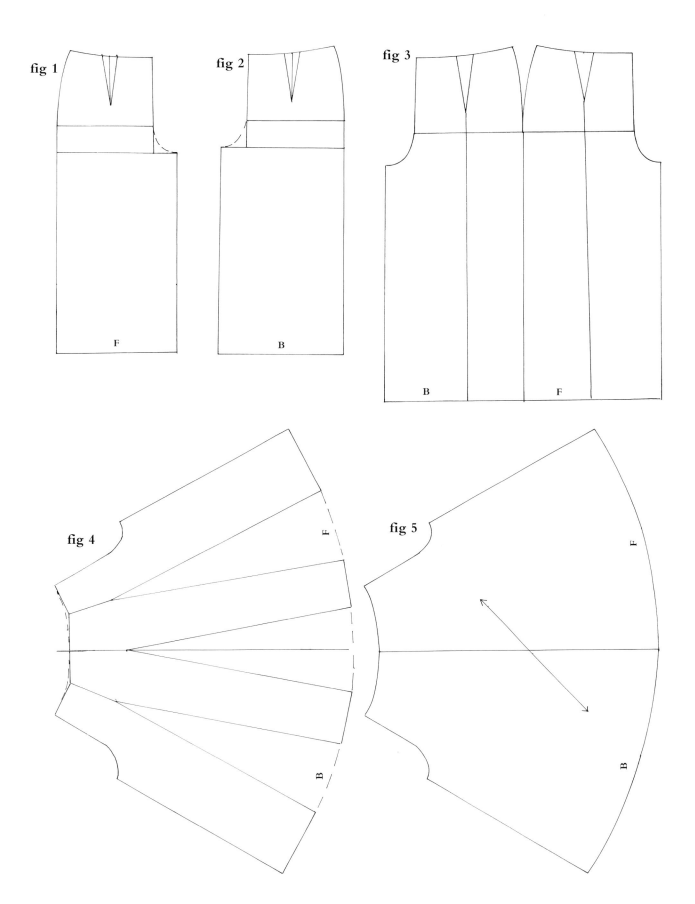

fig 1

fig 2

fig 3

F

B

B

F

fig 4

fig 5

F

B

F

B

Slips and Dresses

Strappy Shift

An equally pretty shape, whether long or short, this shift is ideal for a party dress or a rather glamorous nightdress.

Front and Back

1 For both front and back patterns: trace off lingerie block and lengthen or shorten as desired for the final pattern.
2 Decide where the flare should begin and draw in a flare line, parallel with hip, **figs 1 and 2.**
3 From flare line to hem, divide vertically into equal sections, **figs 1 and 2.**
4 Cut away on flare line and slash up from hem, **fig 3.**
5 Spread the slashed section evenly to give as much fullness as desired, **fig 3.** Do not allow the spread area to overlap upper part of pattern, **fig 3.** The amount of fullness given is a matter of taste but be careful not to skimp. It is essential to cut a calico toile before finalizing your pattern.

6 Draw in new side seam, softening the angle where the two sections meet, **fig 3.**
7 Shorten bust dart by approximately 2.5cm (1 in), **fig 3.**
8 Trace off for final pattern; dot in line for facing pattern, and trace off, **fig 4.** If preferred, the top of the garment may be bound with a bias strip but as the garment itself is bias cut this can lead to the upper edge stretching. A facing cut on the straight grain gives control to the neckline, **fig 5.**
9 The straight grain should be at 45 degrees to the CF and CB line.
10 Make bias-cut rouleau straps and thread cord through to give a rounded finish and prevent stretch.

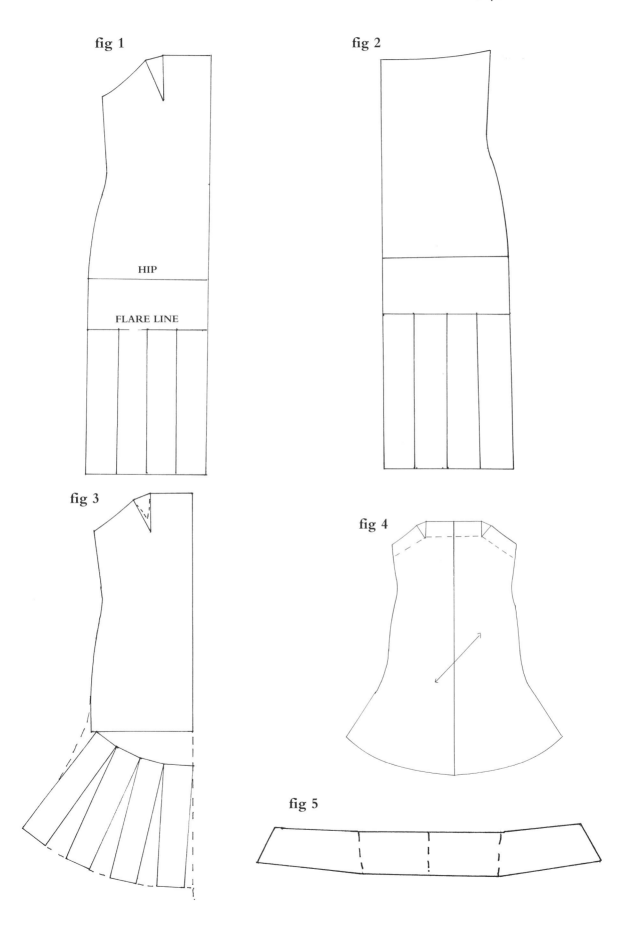

fig 1

HIP

FLARE LINE

fig 2

fig 3

fig 4

fig 5

Empire Line Mini Dress or Nightdress

This is intended to be very loose fitting around the bust. If a closer fit is wanted follow instructions 5–9 for bra-topped slip (nightdress).

Front and Back

1   Outline front and back lingerie blocks and shorten as required. Ignore dent shaping.
2   Add fullness to skirt at hem on side seams and rule back to hip, **figs 1-2.**
3   Draw in style lines for bodice top and put in balance marks, see broken line, **figs 1-2.**
4   Cut away front bodice on style line and place CF line of this section on to fold of paper. Cut and open out for final pattern of whole front (left and right), **fig 3.**
5   Put in balance marks and make straight grain line at 45 degrees to CF line. Cut one in fabric, **fig 3.**

6   For back bodice, repeat steps 4 and 5, **fig 4.**
7   For front skirt, place cut-away section against fold of paper and cut, then open out, **fig 5.** The straight grain lies at 45 degrees to CF line.
8   For back skirt, repeat step 7, **fig 6.**
9   To add extra fullness to skirt, follow instructions for slashing and spreading on strappy shift pattern.

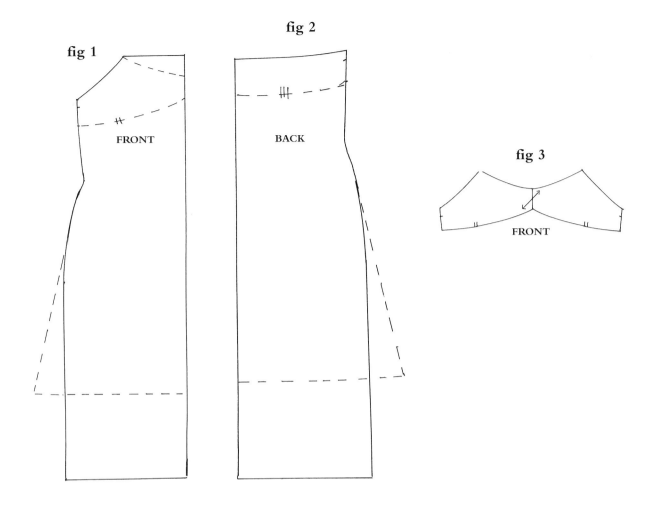

fig 1

FRONT

fig 2

BACK

fig 3

FRONT

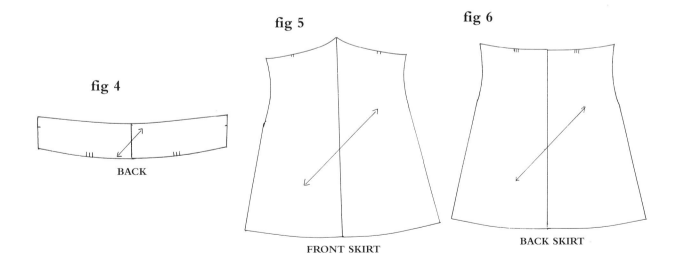

fig 4

BACK

fig 5

FRONT SKIRT

fig 6

BACK SKIRT

Bra-topped Slip or Nightdress

This garment looks and feels wonderful and would be suitable for a simple but elegant wedding dress, perhaps with a stole or jacket.

Front

1 Outline the front lingerie block.
2 Lengthen skirt to mid-calf or ankle, see broken lines, **fig 1.**
3 Dot in hip line.
4 Draw in style line for bra top and put in balance marks, **fig 1.**
5 Cut bra section away on style line, **fig 2a.**
6 On bra, cut open under bust dart from style line to bust point and close out top dart to bust point, **fig 2a.** The opened lower dart forms the gathers.
7 To shorten neckline edge and prevent gaping, angle off from CF line on to neckline by about 1.5cm, (⅝ in) see broken lines, **fig 2a.**
8 The straight grain runs either with CF line or at 45 degrees (true bias), **fig 3.**
9 Ignore the dart on the lower pattern, **fig 2b**, but shave off an equivalent amount on side seam, **fig 2b.**
10 At side seam and CF line hem, add equal fullness, say 1.5cm (⅝ in) and raise at each point by about 2.5mm (¼ in) to curve evenly for hem, **fig 2b.**
11 Measure width at hem and hip to find the centre of the panel and mark in straight grain on this line, **fig 3.** For softer fullness mark straight grain at 45 degrees off this line. Trace off for final pattern and add balance marks at seams.
12 Final patterns, **fig 3.** Cut two of each.

Back

13. Outline the back lingerie block; measure depth of bra top at front side seam, and mark same point on back side seam. Draw in style line to CB and put in balance mark, broken line **fig 4.**
14 Cut away and close back dart out, **fig 5.** Correct line to remove angles, see broken line.
15 Ignore back waist dart, but adjust at side seam as for front pattern, **fig 5.**
16 Follow instructions for adding fullness to skirt from front, steps 9 to 11 above. Trace off for final back patterns, **fig 6.** Cut two of each pattern piece.

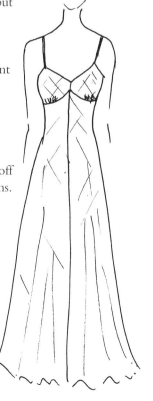
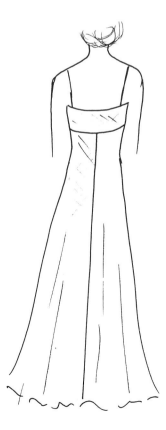

fig 1

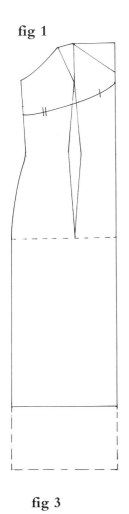

fig 2a

fig 2b

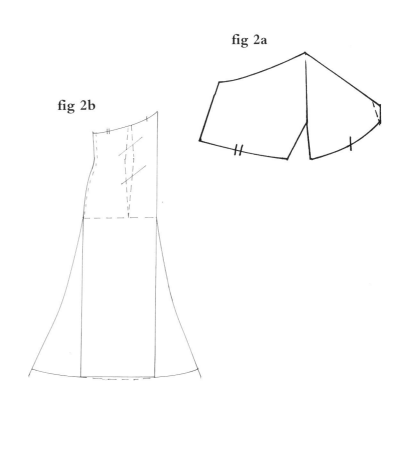

fig 3

fig 4

fig 5

fig 6

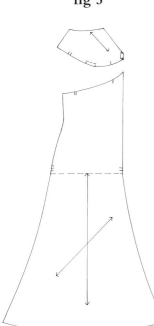

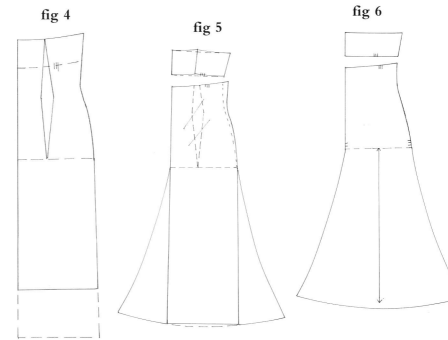

Low-backed Evening Dress

This elegant slim-fitting style looks good on tall slim figures, but also gives a streamlining effect to the shorter curvaceous shapes. Equally attractive in either silk or synthetic crepe de chine or in a fine soft wool, which drapes well. The dress may be cut in jersey fabric with the straight grain to the centre front and back. Contrast fabrics for bodice and skirt also lend themselves to the style. If the back is cut somewhat higher then it makes a good design for a summer nightdress.

Front

1   Trace the front of the lingerie block.
2   Extend the length as required and add fullness to the side seam at the hem, ruling back to skirt, see broken lines, **fig 1.**
3   Shave off on side seam to compensate for some dart shaping not used, see broken line, **fig 1.**
4   Draw in the style line for the bra and put in balance marks, **fig 1.**
5   Cut away the bra section, close out the top dart to bust point, thereby opening the under-bust dart so that the pattern lies flat, **fig 2.** This then gives extra gathering under the bust.
6   Measure the length over the shoulder to the planned upper edge of the garment back and extend for the strap, see broken line, **fig 2.** This may be adjusted when fitting.
7   Take the skirt section of the front garment and place CF line on folded pattern paper, cut through double thickness and open out to whole front. Put in balance marks and grain line at 45 degrees to CF, **fig 3.**

Back

8   Outline the back lingerie block. Extend the length and add fullness, as for front pattern.
9   Measure down the side seam at underarm to check amount lowered on front and take same amount off back pattern. Draw in back curve and shave off at side seam to allow for dart shaping, **fig 4.**
10 Place on fold of paper as for front pattern.
11 Check length of front and back patterns is accurate and ensure all pattern markings are in place.

The bodice of this garment should be fully lined and bagged out (turned through) to enclose under-bust seam. Cut facing or binding for upper edge of back garment.

fig 1

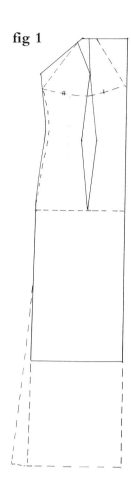

fig 2

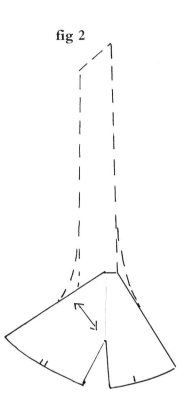

fig 3

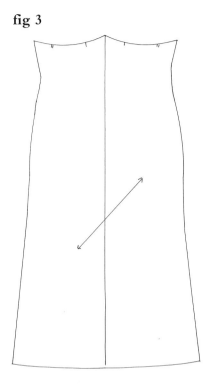

fig 4

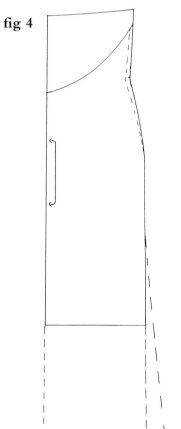

fig 5

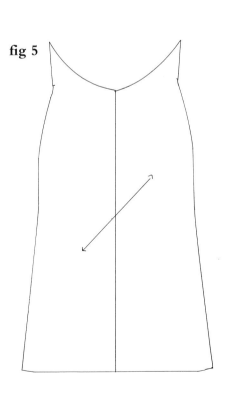

Classic Princess-line Petticoat

This style could also serve as a simple semi-fitted evening dress. For a petticoat, the centre front panel may be cut from lace or contrast jacquard design, plain crepe or satin being used for the other panels.

Front

1   Outline front lingerie block; measure across at hip and hem, and divide width by three.

2   Draw vertical line one third of panel width from CF line, **fig 1.** Put in balance marks across this line.

3   Shift main dart to this line, reducing waist dart size by about 50 per cent, see broken line, **fig 1.**

4   Keeping bust point in position, pivot top of bust dart towards CF, see broken line, **fig 1.**

5   Lengthen or shorten pattern as required.

6   Cut up vertical line, removing dart shaping to the broken line, **fig 2.** Soften angle at bust point on side front panel.

7   On side front pattern add flare equally to both seams from hip to hem, **fig 2.**

8   For CF pattern piece, add flare from hip to hem as for side front; place section on folded paper; cut through double thickness, and open out to full front pattern, **fig 3.** Cut one.

Back

9   Outline back block, shift dart on to line one third of block width and divide as instructed for front patterns, adding flare and balance marks to correspond with front, **figs 4, 5 & 6.**

10 All pattern pieces to be cut with grain at 45 degrees to centre of panel.

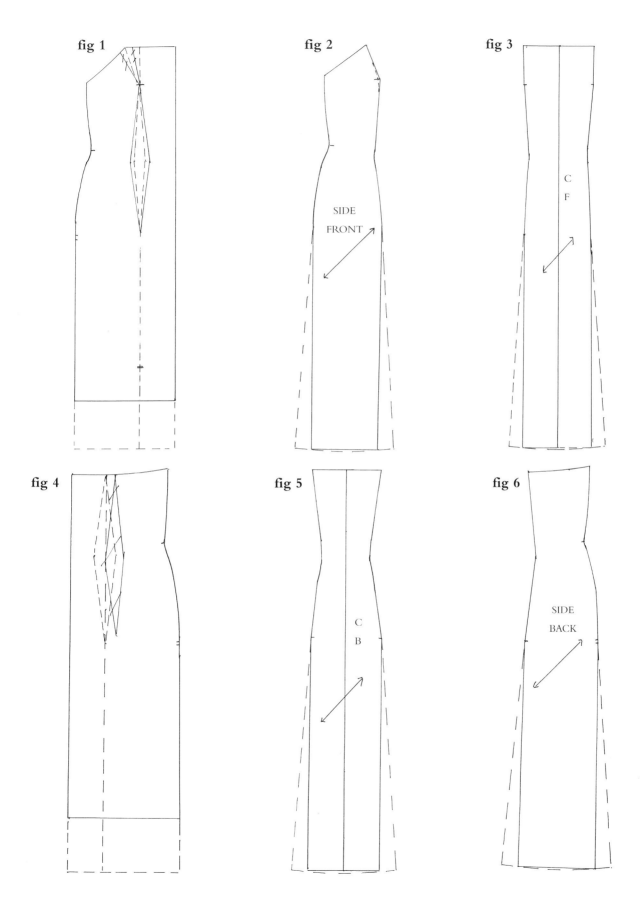

fig 1

fig 2

SIDE

FRONT

fig 3

C
F

fig 4

fig 5

C
B

fig 6

SIDE

BACK

Lace-topped Princess-line Evening Dress

This garment looks good when made with a heavily figured scalloped-edge lace and Jacquard silk.

Front

1 Outline the front lingerie block; shift darts as for the Classic princess-line petticoat and lengthen at hem as needed.
2 Lower CF neckline and draw in style line for lace top through bust point, see broken lines, **fig 1**. Put in balance marks.
3 Cut away top and fold out the dart from bust point to neckline. Straight grain to CF, **fig 2.** This section may be cut either with princess seaming through the dart line, to reflect the rest of the garment, or in one piece.
4 For side front panel, draw horizontal line across hip level and divide lower skirt into equal sections, **fig 3.**
5 Cut across the hip line and cut up all vertical lines on lower skirt. Spread evenly for fullness, making sure that upper and lower sections do not overlap. Soften angles, **fig 4.**
6 Trace off with all markings for final pattern piece, **fig 5.** Cut 2.

7 Cut CF panel on folded paper and open for whole pattern. Cut away at hipline and divide lower section as for side front, **fig 6.**
8 Slash and spread evenly for fullness to match side front, **fig 7.** Trace off for final pattern. Cut 1.

Back

9 Outline block and shift dart as for Classic princess-line petticoat, lengthen to match front pattern, **fig 8.**
10 Lower back neckline and draw in style line for lace top, ensuring match at side seam with front style line, **fig 8.**
11. Follow points 3 to 8 for front pattern. Check all markings are shown and all pattern pieces labelled. Cut one centre back panel and two side back panels.

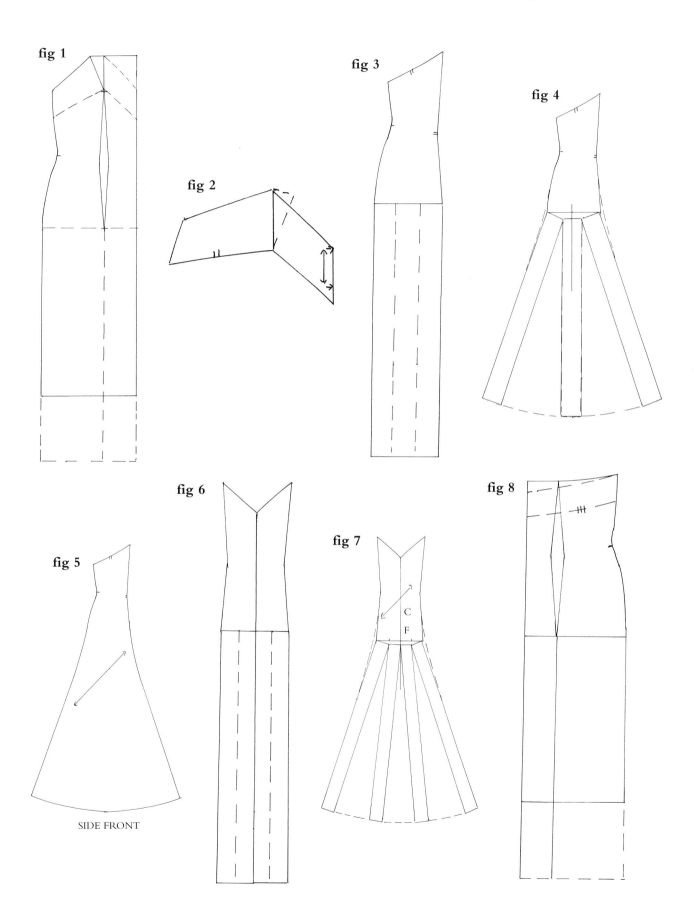

fig 1

fig 2

fig 3

fig 4

fig 5

SIDE FRONT

fig 6

fig 7

C
F

fig 8

Under-wired Bra-topped Slip or Dress

Here is another design that serves equally well as a dress or a slip.

Front

1 Outline the front lingerie block and draw in style lines for bra top, **fig 1.** Put in balance marks, and then cut away bra from skirt.
2 Cut through horizontal style line on bra and close out darts, **fig 2.** The bias grain line runs across the vertical on each section.
3 On the front skirt, remove the waist dart and adjust at side seam as needed, see broken line, **fig 3.**
4 Lengthen the skirt at the hem and add an equal amount of fullness each side. Draw back from hem to hip, **fig 3.**
5 Bind inside of under-bust seam and insert wires.

Back

6 Outline the back block.
7 Match depth of bra top to front at side and draw in the style line for back, **fig 4.** Cut away.
8 Lengthen skirt to equal front. Mark line down centre of panel; add fullness at hem, and rule back to nothing at hip, **fig 5.**
9 On the back bodice pattern, mark the straight grain to CB fold line and cut one in lace. If using a non-stretch fabric cut on the true bias, **fig 6.**
10 It may be necessary to narrow the pattern for a snug fit. If so, shave off a little at the side seams from the upper edge to the hip.

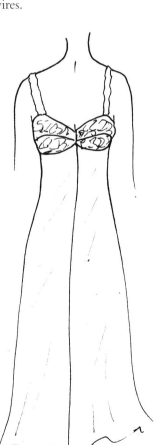

fig 1

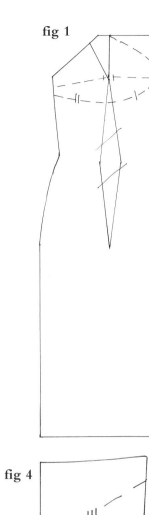

fig 2

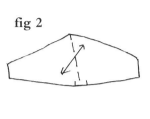

fig 3

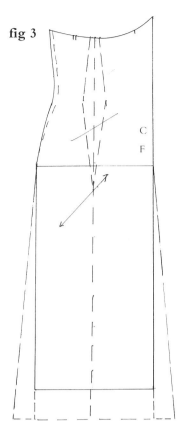

fig 4

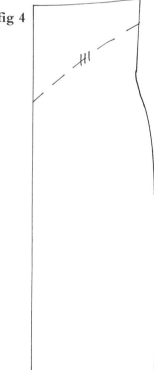

fig 5

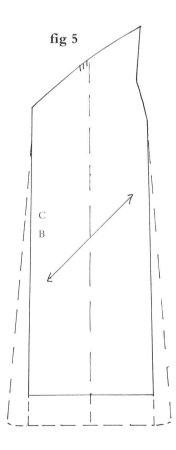

fig 6

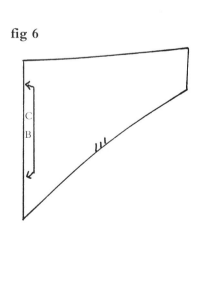

Bias-panelled Dress with Cap Sleeve

This very 1930s dress looks deceptively simple, but it is essential to cut and fit a toile in a suitably draping fabric before cutting the fashion fabric. Copy both blocks over the whole body, left and right.

Front

1   Outline the lingerie block. Lengthen at hem. Delete the waist darts and draw in style lines, putting in balance marks that clearly identify the different panels, **fig 1**. (It is useful to number the panels 1-5.)
2   Cut away section one, cutting away the bust dart on the left side of the bodice, **fig 2**. Soften the angle at the base of dart. This now forms part of the style line.
3   On the right bust dart, open the horizontal style line to the bust point and close the upper dart to compensate, **fig 2**. (Remember when stitching darts that the dressmaker's dart finishes short of the pattern-cutter's dart, see broken line, **fig 3**.)
4   On section two, soften the angle where the left bust dart has been removed, **fig 3**. Sections three and four need only to be separated from those adjoining, **figs 4–5**.
5   Section five forms the flounce at the hem of the skirt. Divide into equal sections and slash up from the lower to upper edge. Do not cut through at the upper edge, **fig 6**.
6   Spread evenly either side of the centre line, **fig 7**, and trace off for final pattern, **fig 8**.
7   Place grain line at 45 degrees from the CF line on all sections.

Back

8   Outline block and draw in line 5cm above the underarm line (upper edge), **fig 9**.
9   Delete waist darts and narrow off at side seams to compensate, **fig 9**.
10 Match the points on both side seams to those of the bias lines on the front pattern and draw in style lines, **fig 9**.
11 From side seams put in style line to meet raised underarm line), **fig 9**.

12 Cut away all sections, putting in balance marks and grain lines as for front.
13 Slash and spread section ten as for section five.

Sleeve

14 Measure across the top of the shoulder from front to back, draw a straight line this length, plus 1cm (2.5cm) for ease. Mark in angles to coincide with front and back bodice at either end and draw cap sleeve approximately 15 to 20 cm (6 to 8 in), at the widest point), **fig 10**. If a fuller sleeve is wanted, slash the outer edge and spread, while keeping the shoulder front to back line the same length as you curve it. If adopting this method, it is wise to tape the inner edge (which goes over the shoulder of the garment) to prevent stretching.

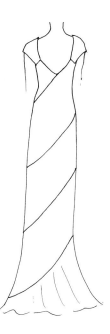

fig 1

fig 3

fig 2

fig 4

fig 5

fig 6

fig 9

fig 10

fig 7

fig 8

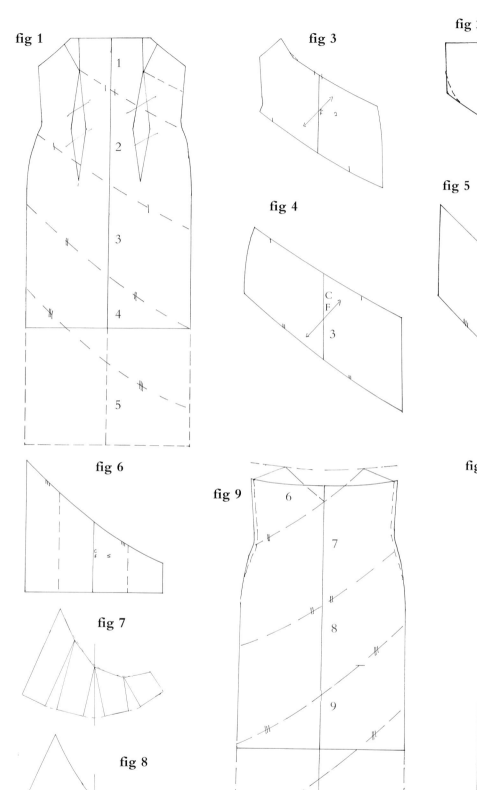

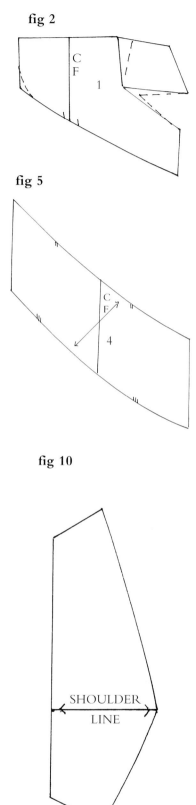

SHOULDER
LINE

Halter-neck Evening Dress

This is a perennial favourite.

Front

1 Outline the lingerie block and lengthen as required, **fig 1.**
2 Draw in deep curved neckline; strike out the waist dart, and shave off at side seam to compensate, **fig 1.**
3 Mark line at right angle from CF to bust point, **fig 1.**
4 Cut away the neck on style line; slash open on horizontal line to bust point, and close vertical dart, see broken line, **fig 2.** This new dart shape forms the CF gathers at bust which will bring the line back to CF.
5 'Grow on' the halter neck, curving off at outer edge to underarm, **fig 2.** Trace off pattern, and mark vertical line half width of hip and half of hem. The grain line lies at 45 degrees to this line, **fig 2.**

Back

6 Outline block, and lengthen to match front pattern. Shift half the waist dart to CB, **fig 3.** Draw in curved style line for back neck, broken line, **fig 3.** Cut away.
7 Trace off pattern and mark grain line as for front, **fig 4.**

fig 1

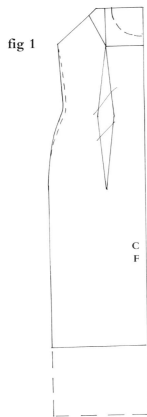

C
F

fig 2

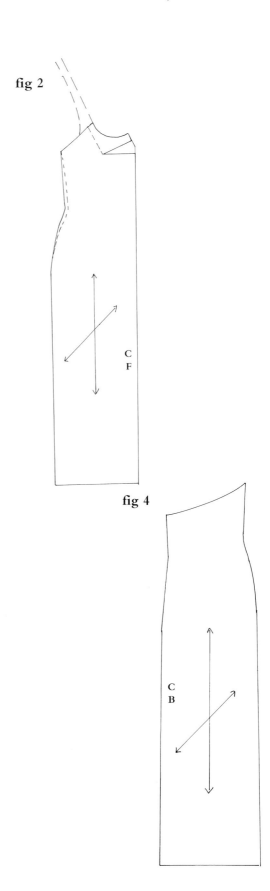

C
F

fig 3

C
B

fig 4

C
B

Easy-to-wear Nightdress

This simple easy-fit style with a front fastening is suitable for a feeding mother. It may be made with or without a frill at the hem. It is pretty made up in broderie anglais or a printed cotton lawn.

Front

1 Outline the lingerie block and draw in the style line for the front neckline. Lengthen as needed, see broken lines, **fig 1.**

2 Separate the bodice from the skirt at the waist. On the bodice, slash through the waist dart to the bust point, close out about half of the small bust dart, **fig 2.** What remains of the dart is used to ease the upper edge into the binding or trimming, **fig 2.**

3 Trace off the front pattern, ignoring the darts, and add a button stand and facing at the centre front, **fig 3.**

4 On the front skirt, square off at the hip curve; remove the waist dart, and draw a vertical line through the centre of the panel, **fig 4.**

5 Slash up from the hem and spread the panel for required fullness, **fig 5.**

6 Redraw and mark the centre of the panel. Mark the true bias across this, **fig 6.**

7 If a frill is wanted at the hem, reduce the length and cut a straight strip twice the width of the skirt, see broken line, **fig 6.**

Back

8 Outline the block and separate bodice and skirt as for the front.

9 On the bodice, ignore the dart shaping and straighten off the side seams, **fig 7.**

10 For the back skirt, follow instructions for the front from steps 4–7.

Trim

11 Make up the bodice and bind the upper edge either with bias binding cut from the fabric or, if the garment is cut from broderie anglais or a similar fabric, use a plain bought nainsook binding. Use a slotted ribbon at the waist to join the bodice and skirt and thread a drawstring through.

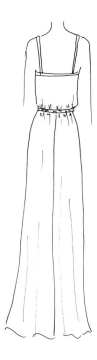

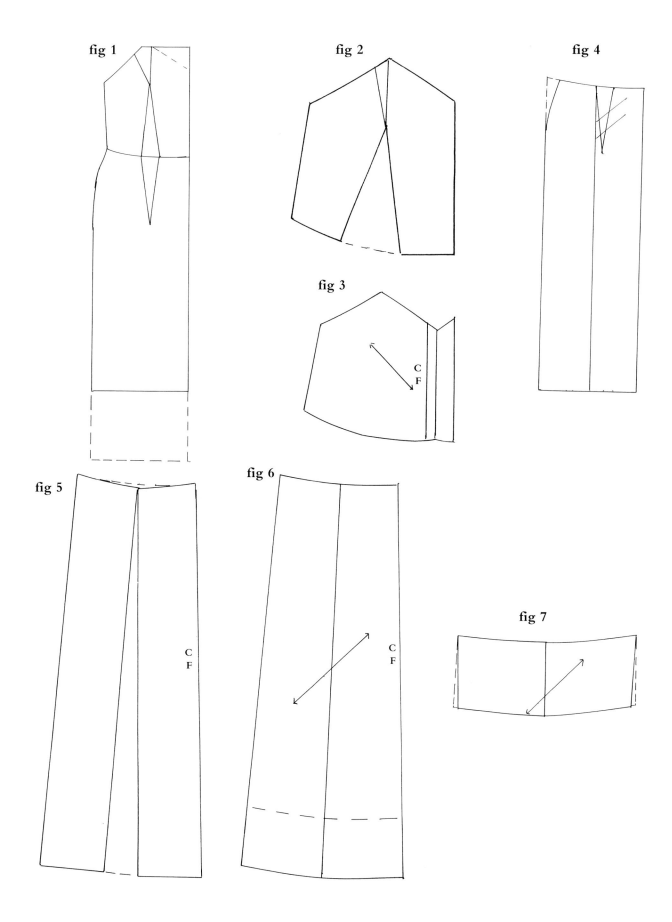

fig 1

fig 2

fig 4

fig 3

C
F

fig 5

C
F

fig 6

C
F

fig 7

Cowl-necked Evening Dress

This gently draped neckline has an everlasting appeal. When cutting a front bodice with a bias cowl, it is wise to cut the back bodice on the straight grain. This gives a little extra control and prevents the garment from slipping off the shoulder.

Front

1 Outline the fitted garment block and draw in style lines at the neck and under the bust. Put in balance marks. Draw a horizontal line from the bust point to the CF line, **fig 1.** Cut away on the style lines and mark in the curves for the cowl from shoulder to CF, see broken lines, **fig 2.**

2 Slash across from CF to the bust point and close out the shoulder dart, **fig 2.** Place the CF on a straight line and draw a right angle off to the shoulder point. Slash through the curves from the CF line to the shoulder and lift the curves, **fig 3.**

3 Trace off the pattern with CF to fold of paper. Fold away paper for the facing along top line. Cut and open out pattern to whole front, **fig 4.**

4 Mark true bias across the CF line, **fig 4.**

5 If a little more shaping is wanted, reduce at the side seam, see broken lines, **fig 4.**

6 Lengthen the skirt as required and mark the centre of the panel from hip to hem. Move the dart to this line, **fig 5.**

7 Slash up the centre line and close out the dart at the under-bust seam line, **fig 6.**

8 It may be necessary to soften the curve at the hip, see broken line, **fig 6.**

9 Trace off on folded paper and open to whole front skirt. Mark the true bias across the CF line and put in balance marks, **fig 7.**

Back

10 Draw in style lines for neck and bodice/skirt seam. Ensure they match the front pattern at shoulder and side seam, **fig 8.**

11 Cut away the bodice and reduce the depth of the neckline at the shoulder, see broken lines, **fig 9.**

12 Draw in a line from the point of the dart to neckline, see broken line, **fig 9.** Slash up dart and pinch out a dart on line from neck, **fig 10.** This shortens the neck edge and prevents gape.

13 Trace off and mark in true bias as for front, **fig 11.** Adjust width at side seam.

14 Follow instructions for the front skirt as above, ensuring that all balance marks are accurately marked.

fig 1

fig 2

fig 3

fig 4

FACING

C
F

fig 5

fig 6

fig 7

C
F

fig 8

fig 9

fig 10

fig 11

C
B

Cowl-necked Shift Dress

This garment is made on the same system as the previous cowl neck, but is cut from an adapted lingerie block.

Front

1   Outline the lingerie block and mark in the lowered neckline and the curves where the cowl folds are wanted, see broken lines, **fig 1.**
2   Cut away the bodice from the skirt at the waist. Cut away the neckline on the style line, **fig 2.**
3   Slash open the curved lines from the CF to the bust point and dart, **fig 2.**
4   Close out the bust dart and close half the waist dart. This lifts and spreads the slashed lines, **fig 2.**
5   Mark a straight line and place the CF against this, **fig 2.**
6   Square off across the top of the folded out bust dart, **fig 2.**
7   Join the bodice pattern back to the skirt at waist, taking care not to overlap, **fig 3.**
8   Soften the curve at the waist side seam to the hip and flare out from hip to hem at the side seam, see broken lines, **fig 3.**
9   Trace off against fold of paper and open out to whole front pattern. The grain line lies at 45 degrees to CF. Curve up slightly at side seam hem, see broken lines, **fig 4.** The straight line across the upper edge falls into a soft cowl shape when worn.

Back

10   Outline the block and delete the darts, **fig 5.**
11   Reduce the pattern at the side seam to reflect half the dart shaping and give a snug fit, **fig 5.**
12   Add flare from hip to hem. Curve back hem to match front.

Dramatic Cowl

13   Take the final front pattern above and raise the upper edge by approximately 5 cm. (2 in), see broken line, **fig 6.** Curve back to underarm.
14   Divide the armhole to upper edge section into three, see broken lines, **fig 7.**
15   Cut down through centre and out to armhole on these lines. Swing out and up thus widening the upper edge, **fig 8.**
16   Draw in straight line across from upper corner to upper corner, **fig 8.** This give a much deeper cowl.
17   Trace off the final pattern and add facing as shown, **fig 9.**

To control the cowl it is useful to stitch small weights in the neckline facing.

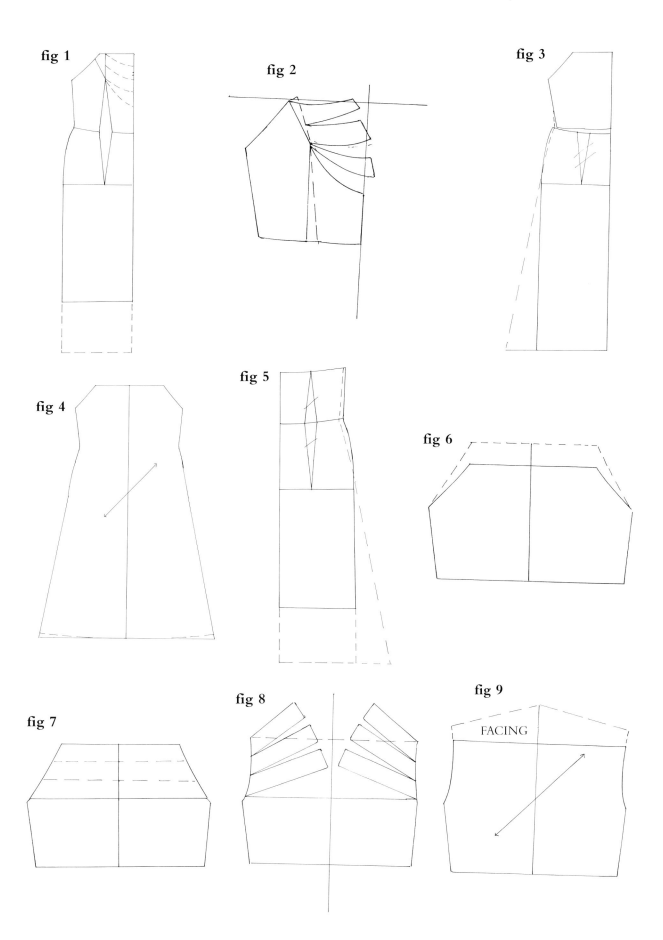

fig 1

fig 2

fig 3

fig 4

fig 5

fig 6

fig 7

fig 8

fig 9

FACING

Basque-waisted Evening Dress

This elegant dress is based on a wonderful black crepe 1930s gown in the Irene Barnes collection at Manor House Museum in Bury St Edmunds, Suffolk. The garment may be made with or without sleeves and with or without the godet (a triangular section added to the skirt). The insertion of a godet gives the possibility of a train, which makes this dress very suitable for a bridal gown.

Front bodice

1   Outline the lingerie block and mark in the style lines, see broken lines, **fig 1**. Put in balance marks.
2   Cut away bodice and slash open under-bust dart to the point. Fold out the shoulder dart, **fig 2**. Lower the shoulder line at the neck edge and draw in a line from the bust point to the neckline, see broken lines, **fig 2**.
3   Pinch a dart into the pattern on the line from bust to neck, thus opening the bust dart further, **fig 3**.
4   This shortens the neck edge and prevents gape. Straighten the neck from shoulder to CF, **fig 3**.
5   Trace off and mark the dart shaping for gathers under the bust. Draw in a line parallel with the original CF and mark the true bias across this, **fig 4**.

Basque

6   Straighten the dart shaping from top to bottom, broken line **fig 5**.
7   Fold out the dart and correct curve, **fig 6**.
8   Trace off with straight grain to the CF, **fig 7**. (When cutting the garment be sure to cut CF to fold.)

Front skirt

9   Lengthen as required and mark the centre of the panel through hip to hem, move the dart to this line, **fig 8**.
10   Slash up centre of the panel, spread hem and close out the dart. Correct seam curve, **fig 9**.
11   Redraw and mark the centre of the panel. Mark the true bias across this, **fig 10**.

Back

12   Mark in the style lines; put in balance marks, and separate the pattern pieces, **fig 11**.
13   Correct the length of the neck edge as for the front bodice, steps 3-5 above, **figs 12, 13, and 14**.
14   On the basque back, close the dart as for the front, **fig 15**.
15   Follow the instructions given for the front skirt for the back, ensuring that the two are spread equally for fullness.
16   If using a **godet**. Measure the seam length on the CB panel and draw an inverted T, solid lines **fig 16**.
17   Measure from the points of the base line to the centre line the length of the CB skirt. Draw this back to the centre to form a triangle. Curve off at the hem and put in the true bias across the centre line, **fig 16**. Always be generous in the width of a godet, they can look skimpy if too narrow.

If using a sleeve ensure it is cut from the same block from which the bodice is drawn.

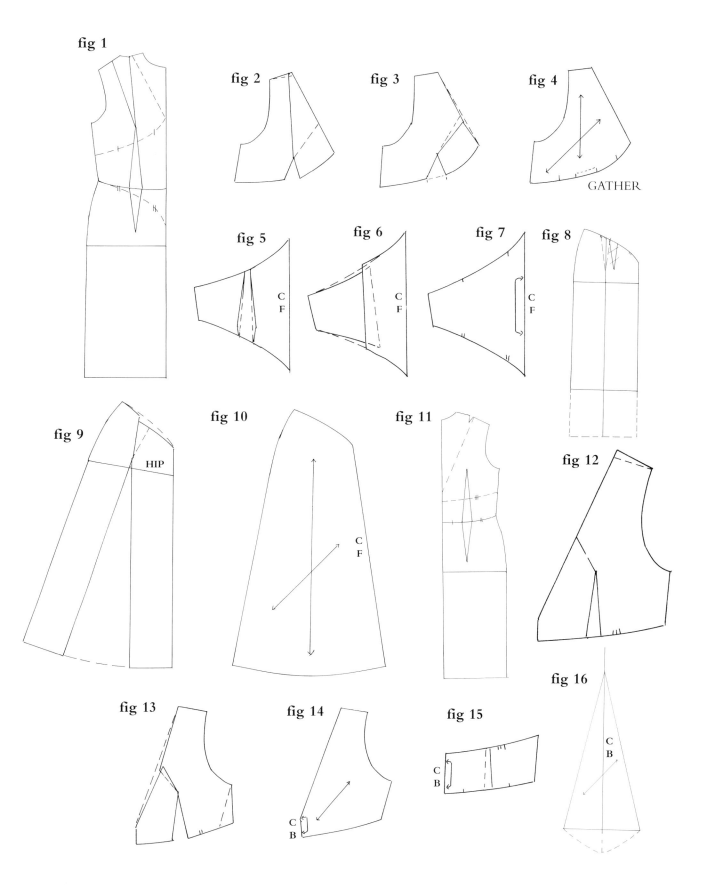

fig 1

fig 2

fig 3

fig 4

GATHER

fig 5

C
F

fig 6

C
F

fig 7

C
F

fig 8

fig 9

HIP

fig 10

C
F

fig 11

fig 12

fig 13

fig 14

C
B

fig 15

C
B

fig 16

C
B

Strapless Evening Dress with Bias-cut Skirt

This is a classic shape. The bodice should be fully lined and bones inserted in the lining along the princess seams. The bodice may have a back fastening, in which case it should be cut with a button stand and facing on the right side and rouleau loops inserted between CB garment and lining on the left back. Otherwise it may be cut with no CB seam on the bodice and a zip in the left side.

Front

1 Outline lingerie bodice and draw in style lines for neckline. Lower the armhole approximately 2 cm (¾ in), see broken lines, **fig 1.**
2 Enlarge bust and waist darts, see broken lines, **fig 1** – a tighter fit is essential for a strapless garment.
3 Cut away bodice and cut away on the dart lines, making a centre front panel and a side front panel. Soften the angle at the bust point, **fig 2.** The centre front panel may be cut as one with CF to the fold or as two with a centre seam.
4 Put in balance marks.
5 Lengthen the skirt, see broken lines, **fig 1.**
6 Reduce width on hip curve and make the waist dart smaller, **fig 3.**
7 Widen skirt at side seam hem and rule back to the hip, see broken line, **fig 3.**
8 Trace off with CF to fold of paper and open out. Mark true bias across CF line, **fig 4.** If a fuller skirt is used, it is possible to eradicate the waist dart by slashing up to the point and closing the dart, thus widening the skirt at the hem.

Back

9 Outline the block and lower across to match the front pattern at armhole edge, **fig 5.**
10 Narrow off bodice at the side seam, see vertical broken line, **fig 5.**
11 Increase width of dart at the waist, **fig 5.**
12 Cut away the bodice from the skirt and separate side back from centre back by cutting away the dart completely, **fig 6.** If CB fastenings are required, add a button stand and facing to the right side, see broken lines, **fig 6.**. Otherwise the CB may be cut to the fold of fabric.
13 For the back skirt, follow steps 6–9 as for the front skirt, **figs 7–8.**

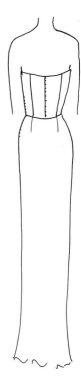

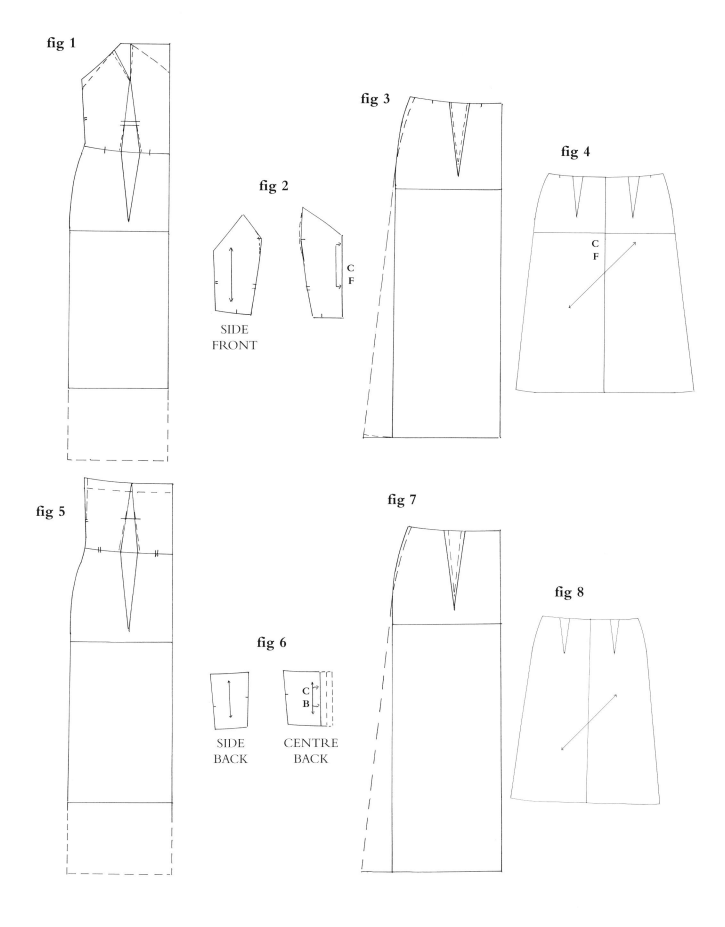

fig 1

fig 2

SIDE
FRONT

C
F

fig 3

fig 4

C
F

fig 5

fig 6

SIDE
BACK

CENTRE
BACK

C
B

fig 7

fig 8

Two-fabric Slip or Dress

A deceptively simple design, this is very flattering to most figures. The contrast trim should be cut double and bagged out like a yoke over the seam line of the skirt. It looks good with a satin trim and crepe de chine skirt.

Front

1 Outline the lingerie block and mark in the style lines. Put in balance marks. Strike out the waist dart, **fig 1.** Adjust side seam to compensate for removal of the dart and give some shaping (as in **fig 6**).
2 Trace off the trim section and close out the bust dart, **fig 2.** Place CF on fold of paper and cut double, open out to whole front, **fig 2.**
3 Trace off the skirt section, mark in the hip line and mark vertical line through centre of hip to hem. Draw the true bias line across this, **cut 2, fig 3.**

Back

4 Outline the block and mark in style lines, ensuring that the depth of the trim matches the front on the side seam, **fig 4.**
5 Cut away the trim. Ignore the dart but measure off an equal amount at the side seam, **fig 5.** Place CB on fold of paper and cut double. The grain line runs across the CB line, **fig 5.**
6 On the skirt section strike out the dart, but curve in slightly at the side seam to compensate and give some shaping, **fig 6.**
7 Mark centre of the panel and put in true bias across this, **fig 6.**

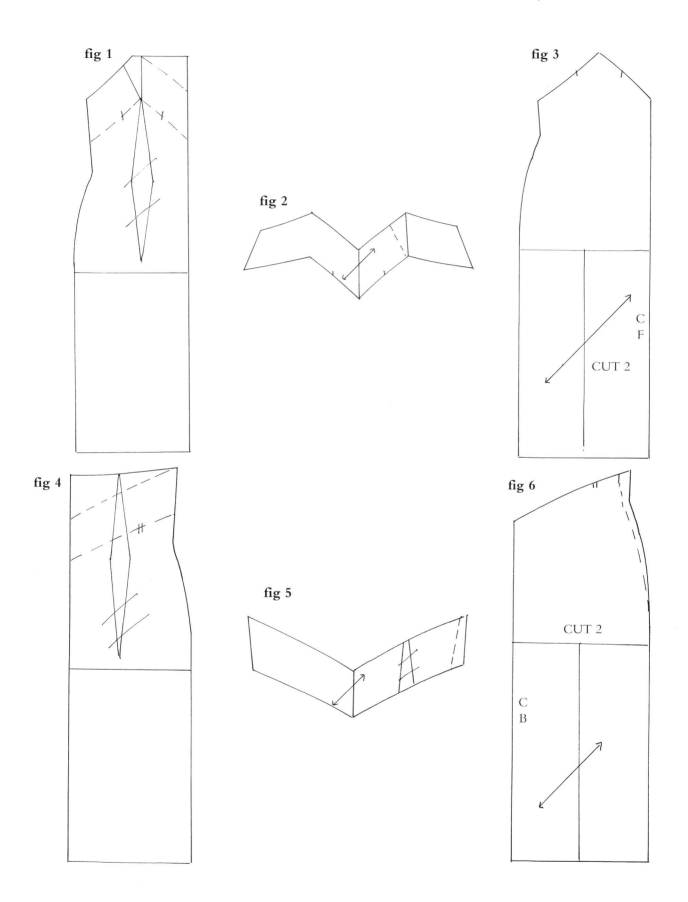

fig 1

fig 2

fig 3

C
F

CUT 2

fig 4

fig 5

fig 6

CUT 2

C
B

Bra-topped Dress with Flounced Skirt

Equally attractive as a formal dress or a nightdress, the success of this pattern depends on the fabric chosen.

Front

1 Outline the front lingerie block and lengthen as required. Lower the armhole on the side seam and draw in the bra and the flounce style lines, see broken lines, **fig 1.** Put in balance marks.

2 Cut away the bra on style lines and open the under-bust dart to the point, closing out the top dart, **fig 2.** This provides the gathers or pleats under the bust. Draw a vertical line through the bust point and mark in the true bias across this, **fig 2.**

3 On the body, mark in on the side seam the width at the top of the dart and curve off down to the hip, **fig 3.**

4 Do not make too snug at the waist or this will create unattractive creasing when the wearer sits. Delete the dart, **fig 3.**

5 Trace off the full front on folded paper; open out, and mark in grain line at 45 degrees to the CF, **fig 4.**

6 Divide the flounce in four equal sections; slash up from the hem, and spread out to ¼ circle, **figs 5–6.**

7 Trace off full front flounce and put in grain line, **fig 7.**

Back

8 Lower at the side seam to match the front and curve off the CB, **fig 8.**

9 Reduce the width at the side seam as in step 3 for the front, **fig 8.**

10 Draw in the flounce style line, cut away and slash and spread as for the front, **fig 8.**

11 Trace off the whole back on folded paper and open out, **fig 9.**

fig 1

fig 2

fig 3

fig 5

fig 4

C
F

fig 6

fig 8

fig 9

C
B

fig 7

Equipment and Suppliers

Pattern drafting and cutting, like any other skill, is easier and more successful with the correct tools. It is well worth investing in the following equipment:

• Pattern paper, either plain or dot and cross. Plain paper in single sheets, available from MacCulloch & Wallis (address below), is often more convenient to handle. Dot and cross is usually only available in rolls, which makes it heavy to lift.

• Mounting card or stiff craft paper for making the final blocks.

• Fine line drawing pens. Once the pattern is correct, marking should be in ink so that it does not rub off.

• A selection of pencils and a rubber.

• Metre stick, marked with metric and imperial measurements.

• Dressmakers or 'french' curve.

• Grader set square with metric measurements shown both sides of centre.

• 'Notcher', for putting in balance marks.

• Scissors that are easy to handle when cutting paper. They must give a clean cut. Do No use dressmaking scissors.

• Craft knife, for cutting card.

Most of the necessary items are available by post from:

MacCulloch & Wallis Ltd
25 Dering Street
London W1R 0BH
Tel: 020-7629-0311

Morplan Ltd
PO Box 54
Temple Bank
Harlow
Essex CM20 2TS
Tel: 01279 435333

or 56 Great Titchfield Street
London W1P 8DX
Tel: 020-7636-1887

R.D. Franks Ltd
Market Place
London W1N 8EJ
Tel: 020-7636-1244

R.D. Franks stocks a comprehensive range of books and magazines for fashion students.